"The words 'presence,' 'awareness,' and 'encounter' have experienced a vogue reappearance in recent years. But who is explaining these esoteric and ethereal concepts? My friend David Benner, that is who. In his probing, yet down-to-earth style, David gives us more insight into a spirituality that is at once contemporary and ancient. His work is winsome and practical; he explains and captivates like few can on topics this rich. If you have followed Benner's work you will love this project. If this is your first book, you are in for a feast!"

—**Ron Martoia**, Transformational Architect
(www.RonMartoia.com)

"This book is a profound articulation of how the Divine Spirit pervades all things in the universe: the life force in all living things, the spirit that takes the form of our own spirits within us, and the energy that keeps the electrons in orbit in the atoms of a rock. This all-pervasive Spirit is what Jesus promised in John 14 when he said in effect, 'The age of Jesus Christ is over. Now comes the age when God is a Presence as Spirit.' *Presence and Encounter* clearly illumines our possibilities to be such a Presence to ourselves and each other that we experience in our encounters not just the dynamics of personalities but the numinous *Presence* of God."

—**J. Harold Ellens**, author of *Light from the Other Side: The Paranormal as Friend and Familiar (Real Life Experiences of a Spiritual Pilgrim)*

"*Presence and Encounter* immediately draws a reflective reader into the essence of human living. It exquisitely points toward the possibilities of being totally engaged with all that is present in each moment—being available without reservation to oneself, to others, and to the Loving Presence that holds all. It is filled with joyous invitations to explore."

—**Jeannette A. Bakke**, author of *Holy Invitations: Exploring Spiritual Direction*, spiritual director, teacher, and retreat leader

Books by David G. Benner

Spirituality and the Awakening Self: The Sacred Journey of Transformation (2012)

Soulful Spirituality: Becoming Fully Alive and Deeply Human (2011)

Opening to God: Lectio Divina and Life as Prayer (2010)

Desiring God's Will: Aligning Our Hearts with the Heart of God (2005)

The Gift of Being Yourself: The Sacred Call to Self-Discovery (2004)

Surrender to Love: Discovering the Heart of Christian Spirituality (2003)

Strategic Pastoral Counseling: A Short-Term Structured Model, 2nd ed. (2003)

Sacred Companions: The Gift of Spiritual Friendship and Direction (2002)

Free at Last: Breaking the Bondage of Guilt and Emotional Wounds (1998)

Care of Souls: Revisioning Christian Nurture and Counsel (1998)

Money Madness and Financial Freedom: The Psychology of Money Meanings and Management (1996)

Choosing the Gift of Forgiveness: How to Overcome Hurts and Brokenness, with Robert Harvey (1996)

Understanding and Facilitating Forgiveness, with Robert Harvey (1996)

Counseling as a Spiritual Process (1991)

Healing Emotional Wounds (1990)

Psychotherapy and the Spiritual Quest (1988)

Therapeutic Love: An Incarnational Interpretation of Counseling (1985)

Books Edited by David G. Benner

Spiritual Direction and the Care of Souls: A Guide to Christian Approaches and Practices, with Gary Moon (2004)

Baker Encyclopedia of Psychology and Counseling, 2nd ed., with Peter Hill (1999)

Christian Perspectives on Human Development, with LeRoy Aden and J. Harold Ellens (1992)

Counseling and the Human Predicament: A Study of Sin, Guilt, and Forgiveness, with LeRoy Aden (1989)

Psychology and Religion (1988)

Psychotherapy in Christian Perspective (1987)

Christian Counseling and Psychotherapy (1987)

PRESENCE *and* ENCOUNTER

THE SACRAMENTAL POSSIBILITIES OF EVERYDAY LIFE

DAVID G. BENNER, PhD

BrazosPress

a division of Baker Publishing Group
Grand Rapids, Michigan

© 2014 by David G. Benner

Published by Brazos Press
a division of Baker Publishing Group
P.O. Box 6287, Grand Rapids, MI 49516-6287
www.brazospress.com

Printed in the United States of America

Library of Congress Cataloging-in-Publication Data is on file at the Library of Congress, Washington, DC.

ISBN 978-1-58743-361-0

14 15 16 17 18 19 20   7 6 5 4 3 2 1

To
My brother
Colin James Benner
(1951–2014)
Always a luminous presence
Still a luminous presence

CONTENTS

FOREWORD

I am sincerely happy and honored to write a few words in support of this valuable book. As David Benner so often does,
he moves us toward the heart of the matter with both skill and
simplicity. He knows that the deep and needed transmission in
the world of spirituality takes place through *presence*. That is
indeed the heart of the matter.

Jesus said that he was "present" whenever two or three people
were gathered in the Christ spirit (Matthew 18:20). We Catholics
fervently believe in the doctrine of the "Real Presence" of Jesus
in the physical elements of bread and wine. And Paul even seems
to think that the presence of the Risen Christ, or the Spirit, is the
very engine of consciousness and evolution (Romans 8:16–23).

Now, in our lifetime, scientists are finding ever newer evidence
for what some religious people called *presence* in the very or-
ganizing energy of the universe—from fractals, to holograms,
to electro-magnetism, to force fields, to gravitation itself—all
of which invite us into a certain degree of mystery and non-
explainability—and also participation! The great scientists are
revealed in their contentment to live provisionally with a certain

degree of mystery! I wish we clergy were as patient. We seem to like certainty and answers—now. In our too literal attempts to explain and control presence, we often explain it away, and most people just lose interest in the deeper journey because they are told, in effect, that there is no "deeper" to be had!

Meanwhile, the scientists still search for the pattern behind the patterns, the seeming *vibrational fields that hold all things together.* We from the religious world often call these vibrational fields the divine presence or perhaps the Holy Spirit. As usual, religion intuits and gives metaphor to what science is now confirming and illustrating on ever new verifiable levels. Remember, truth is one (Ephesians 4:4–5) and will necessarily and in time be seen from different angles and at different levels—with ever more appreciation. How blessed we are to live in our time! There are, however, few teachers who can honor the different levels at the same time.

Although we Catholics would never think of denying the doctrine of the Real Presence (because it is the one central mystery of Incarnation continued in space and time), we fail to communicate it at the needed depth to individual believers. It remains what Jesus called "a lesson memorized." This happens largely because we fail to point out that presence is *inherently a relational concept.* Presence demands both a subject and an object existing in mutual respect and expectation (which actually makes the object into another dignified subject!). This is what happened when Francis of Assisi grants even "Brother Sun," "Sister Water," and "Our Sister, Mother Earth" subjectivity, dignity, and reciprocity. This is the genius of mystics, saints, and often poets, and why they keep growing and expanding. But it should be the genius of all believers.

We Catholics usually teach just one side of the equation—the objective presence in the bread and wine—but we often fail to teach the observing subject how he or she can also be present to the Divine Presence that is always seeking to reveal itself! This is *God in Search of Man*, as Abraham Heschel put it in his brilliant book title. This is the absolute importance and centrality of the contemplative mind. The merely functional, problem-solving mind is largely incapable of experiencing any actual real presence.

It is no surprise that David is a teacher—and exemplar—of such contemplative seeing and listening. He could never have written such a fine book unless he was, first of all, a seer himself— for thus he knows how to *enjoy* the vibrational fields of a Loving Presence behind and within the world of things. *This imbedded life and intelligence* pervades the whole universe and all of creation, the mystic says. All elements and animals seem to live inside of this presence quite naturally, all happily obedient to their lovely destiny. Only one species resists and even denies the Presence, and that is us. Don't let it be you!

Richard Rohr, OFM
January 2014
Center for Action and Contemplation
Albuquerque, New Mexico

PREFACE

Far from being merely a topic that I chose out of a desire to write another book, what follows is the fruit of a haunting interest that chose me over forty years ago. I have been pondering the nature of presence and encounter since first reading Martin Buber's *I and Thou* as a university student. His assertion that "All real living is meeting"[1] struck a deeply resonant chord in me. I recognized even then—and now know with much more certainty—that the most vital and significant moments in life are moments of encounter. Whether it is encounter with others, the Wholly Other, or myself, these are moments when I know that life is its own meaning.

Presence makes encounter possible. It also makes life meaningful. The search for meaning is really a search for presence, because grand systems of truth or meaning can never satisfy the basic human longing for life to be meaningful. Without presence, nothing is meaningful. But in the luminous glow of presence, all of life becomes saturated with significance.

Only in presence can we encounter anyone or anything. Others may be present to us, but we will not notice their presence until we are present ourselves. Once we are truly present, everything that has being becomes potentially present to us.

It was a glimpse of these possibilities, along with an encounter with Jung and Freud, that led me into clinical psychology. That same glimpse subsequently guided my efforts to make presence and encounter central to my psychotherapy, spiritual guidance, and transformational coaching. Usually, there has been a gap between my aspirations and my experience, but I have never lost my conviction that all real living is meeting, and that this is made possible by presence.

Yet instrumental applications of these powerful dynamics miss the point that in order to truly unpack transformational potential, presence must be a way of living, not merely something we attempt to do. Presence is not something that can be turned on and off like a tap. It is either an expression of our being or it is posturing and pretense.

Ultimately, we can no more control presence than we can control our being. Presence and being are so beyond our control that we are unable to even adequately define them. I will do my best to clarify what I mean by these terms, but you will quickly notice how big concepts such as *presence* and *being* resist containment in a string of words that we might offer as a definition. This is even more the case when we encounter them with an initial capital letter. When I speak of "Being" or "Presence," I refer to God. Naming the deity in these ways reminds us that neither names nor definitions contain reality but merely and imperfectly point toward it. This is particularly true when words are used to point toward the Ultimate Reality we have conventionally called God. While these concepts are big, it is equally true that they have immense practical implications. It is these implications that most interest me, and we will keep them very much in focus as we explore this topic together.

I long to live with more presence. I long to know the presence of God more deeply. I long to learn how to make myself more available for encounter, and I am convinced that these things are all connected—that somehow my presence is essential to an encounter with the presence of anyone or anything, especially the presence of the One who is the ground of being and the source, therefore, of presence.

I write about these things not so much to communicate what I understand as to help me learn to live with more presence. Consequently, the voice with which I will be writing is a voice of one sharing ponderings rather than teaching truths. It is my hope that my ponderings will evoke your own, for it is in such reflection that the practical implications of the things we discuss will take root in your soul.

Presence requires inner space, and talk about presence requires the same. If, therefore, you are willing to allow these concepts to get you rather than you simply getting them, I would encourage you to make space for reflection. Read the leaf you encountered at the end of the last paragraph as an invitation to pause for reflection. When you come across these leaves throughout the text, stop reading for a moment and be hospitable to your thoughts. Allow yourself to experience the truth of what you have read—or notice how my words fail to capture a truth you know and that I seem to have missed. I will end each chapter with one more chance for "Pausing to Ponder" before we move on, and, of course, you should also pause for reflection at any point that seems to invite it.

Another way you can create inner space and be a good host to the concepts I will be presenting and you will be entertaining is to read soulfully rather than just mentally. Bring your senses and imagination to what I share. Listen with your feelings and pay attention to your body and spirit as you do so. Be attentive to movements within your depths as you engage with the things we will discuss—notice what makes your spirit soar with hope and vitality or what leads you to a place of disquiet; pause and ponder the significance of these inner responses.

Allow our journey together to be a dialogue—not simply between you and me but also within yourself. This will provide the necessary inner space and stillness to allow you to be grasped by truths that can't be grasped by the mind, even though they can be known by the soul.

Lima, Peru
Semana Santa (Holy Week) 2013

1

The Nature
of Presence

The world is full of presence. Every moment of life is crammed full of potential encounters with people and things that are present to us even though we may not be present to them:

- the presence of a city—vital, decaying, dangerous, enchanting, oppressive, perhaps even seductive

- the comforting presence of loved ones—long unseen, sometimes long dead

- the troubling presence of people with whom we have unfinished business

- the evocative presence of a sacred space—perhaps a cathedral, a grove of trees, a shore's edge, or wherever we are called into awareness of the transcendent

- the distinctive presence of a home—immediately noticeable on entering, if we are paying attention

- the unmistakable presence of death that we might experience at a funeral

- the plethora of presences that confront us on entering an art gallery, walking through a shopping mall, or attending to sea life in a tidal pool

- the numinous presence of the Wholly Other—both at times and in places that might be expected but also at times and in places and ways never expected

- the puzzling presence of someone we encounter—disturbing us in ways that may be good or bad but that cannot easily be ignored

What is this strange thing called presence? Presence is the awakening that calls us into an engagement with some aspect of the present moment. Presence makes us feel alive, or, perhaps better, it lets us know that we are alive. It demands that we notice, and, in so doing, the distance between whatever we notice and us is suddenly reduced. We feel connected. Sometimes this might feel like more connection than is comfortable, but no longer are we on the outside looking at life through a thick glass. Suddenly, we have passed through that which distanced us, and we are inside and a part of life. We are involved. We are participants, not simply spectators.

Presence is elusive, but it can come to us with astounding force. Notice how a wisp of a scent can pull us into the presence of a beloved—a presence that may be both subtle yet powerfully real. A great work of music can similarly draw us into the presence of the artist—often into a period of time and a world dramatically different from our own. An experience might invite us to be present to the world and to ourselves. A fleeting memory might instantly draw us into awareness of the absence of one still powerfully present to us.

Sometimes the presence of another commands our attention

and demands our own presence. The Gospels tell the story of Jesus teaching in the temple, and they describe those hearing him as being astounded because he taught as one having authority.[1] What was the basis of that sense of authority? I can't imagine that it came from polished delivery, command of his material, highly developed rhetorical skills, self-confidence, or any other personality trait or thing that he was doing. It sounds to me like the authority of presence.

I recall a silent retreat my wife and I led for a group of advanced contemplatives. Many were nuns and monks, and all had well-developed practices of contemplative prayer and meditation. As I stood before them for an initial teaching session, I was struck by their stillness, openness, and attentiveness. All seemed to belong in this room of invited attendees, but one person particularly caught my attention. There was nothing remarkable about either her appearance or behavior, but something in her way of being suggested what I can only describe as a fierce presence. She seemed to be fully in the present moment—free of inner preoccupations or distractions and capable, therefore, of being unusually open, still, and engaged. I found her presence to be comforting and disturbing, attractive and terrifying. She did not have to speak to have authority; her authority, or power, did not appear to come from anything she did but from who she was. I simply knew that I was in the presence of someone who was fully present to me. That awareness served to deepen my own presence. While there was nothing frightening about her as a person, the intensity and alignment of her being were disarmingly different from the sort of diluted presence I was used to in others and myself.

Presence can be like that. When it is even relatively unclouded, it can shine with a brightness that can be disturbing. But what a good disturbance it is. It is like an alarm going off. It is an invitation to awaken and be present. Its authority is troubling only when we want to remain asleep!

◊

There is something magical about presence. It is not subject to the ordinary laws of materiality and time. Our presence enters the room before we do and often stays long after we leave. When in the presence of someone who is fully present to us, time seems to slow down. Sometimes, it even seems to stop. For a moment, we may feel that there is no past and no future. Physical and emotional distance also seem to collapse in presence. We might feel close to someone who is far away or intimate with a just-encountered stranger. Boundaries between self and others soften and sometimes seem to dissolve, leading to a sense of shared oneness similar to what people sometimes report experiencing in orgasm. The mystics speak much of this sense of oneness and seem incapable of talking about it without the use of the imagery of sexual union.

Presence instantly moves us into a strange place that has an unreal quality to it. Yet in our depths, we know that what we are experiencing is more real than anything we encounter in ordinary consciousness. Presence can be dramatic, but it can also be remarkably ordinary. It can be calming, but, as we have seen, it can also be disturbing. It can be confused and confusing, but it can also possess a luminosity and clarity that lights up a room and can light up a life.

Ralph Harper suggests that "From theophanies to erotic closeness, presence feels the same, even if the personalities are not the same."[2] This also reflects the mysterious nature of presence, in that the clearer the presence of a person, the less it is simply *that* person's presence that we are experiencing. There is something transpersonal about presence. It is as if we are not experiencing the presence of a unique individual but of Presence itself.

Notice how someone can offer us a clear and luminous presence, yet we might know nothing, or almost nothing, about him or her. If we are fortunate enough to subsequently be able to get to know this person better, we may then become aware of two almost separate realities that are present when we are together. We might, on the one hand, continue to encounter the presence that the person radiates, and this may be quite unchanged by knowing things about the person. On the other hand, we can be clearly aware of the person's uniqueness, or what we might call personality. A person's presence will always be less differentiated and more global than his or her personality. It is as if the presence is less "owned" than it is Presence mediated.

When I think of this distinction between encountering a person in his or her uniqueness and encountering the presence that individuals carry and share, I think again of the nun I met in the silent retreat I just described. After this retreat, I had a chance to spend time with this woman, and since then we have become very good friends. In these subsequent interactions, I have come to know much more about her. When we are together now, I can readily see her in her uniqueness and individuality, but I also still powerfully experience the presence she possesses that is not simply hers or about her. The two operate on different planes of reality. Each involves a different level or type of knowing. My knowing of her is shaped by information she has shared about herself and my experiences with her. This grows and changes as the relationship develops. But beneath it, I am always aware of the Presence that I continue to meet in her. This, I know, is not simply reducible to her personality or behavior. It is grounded in her being and made possible by her way of being in relationship to the transcendent Presence she mediates.

These mysteries of presence render it resistant to exhaustive analysis. As with all transcendent realities, while it can never be fully understood, there is no question it can be deeply known.

Everything and everyone has presence. Just think of your experience of things and people when you step back from your thoughts about them. Think, for example, of the presence of a building you are familiar with, perhaps where you work or some place you frequently visit. Notice how the presence of this place may be related to its design and aesthetics but isn't limited to it. Or think of people you regularly encounter, and notice the presence they emanate—not simply their behaviors or their personalities but the auras they give off.

Martin Heidegger said that being is presence.[3] Whatever else this means, it suggests that in some way presence is a basic property of simply being. Everything that exists has presence by virtue of its being.

Being is more straightforward for rocks, trees, and black holes than it is for humans. Inanimate objects are never tempted by false ways of being. They are aligned within their being, and consequently their presence is less ambiguous. This is also true for nonhuman living beings—for example, animals and trees—all of which remain closer to their natures than is true for most humans. As a result, their presence is also more pure and singular.

For humans, living our truth is much more of a challenge. First, we are profoundly alienated from our being. We forget what it is to stand in awe of being itself, and of our being in particular. We are lost in doing and tempted to believe that there is nothing more to us than this. This separation from our being also reflects our separation from Being itself. At the core of our soul is an ache that is answered only in knowing both our being and the Ground of Being. But that ache is easily ignored and misinterpreted, and consequently we seldom are aware of this most fundamental level of our alienation.

A second way that living the truth of our being is more complicated for humans than for nonhumans is that humans alone have the capacity to create false ways of being. As children, we learn to try on various identities as we attempt to discover a satisfactory way of being in the world. Even though we usually lose awareness of doing this after adolescence or early adulthood, we continue to try and create our "self" through the first half of life. But the self we create is a persona—a mixture of the truth of our being and the fictions we spin as we attempt to create a self in the image of an inner fantasy. The simple truth of our being gets lost in the metanarratives we spin. We become the fictions we live. Consequently, our way of being in the world is so false and unnatural that our presence is thoroughly ambiguous. It is no wonder that we find the presence of most people so clouded as to be not worth noticing, and it is no wonder that a truly unclouded presence is so luminous and so compellingly noteworthy!

One final thing to note at this point about the nature of presence is how it lifts us above the sphere of particularities and separateness into a world of integral wholeness. Presence is experienced as a unitary whole. Think, for example, about the experience of sitting on the top of a hill, far from the polluting lights of a city, gazing at a dark, starry sky. Unless you are an astrophysicist or an astronomy buff, your experience will not likely be one of thought and analysis but of singular, holistic absorption. You will experience the presence of the starry sky, not your thoughts about it.

The more pure and uncontaminated the presence, the more it is experienced as a whole. The power of presence seems to gather up all the separate and isolated parts that normally are our focus and wrap itself within a harmonious whole. Complexity is enclosed within a shroud of singularity and wholeness.

Often this sense of wholeness brings with it a surprising sense of increased vividness to everything being experienced—possibly a sense of being more present to your experience, even to yourself. Sometimes this includes a sense of being at one within yourself. Occasionally, this sense of oneness may even include the person who offers the presence (or others who share it), possibly even involving a sense of oneness with everything that is. Frequently, it produces a sense of intimacy that strains the usual subject / object duality. Such an experience might also leave you in awe before the mystery of life; and because it frequently leaves you feeling more whole and integrated, it often feels like an experience of standing on sacred ground. Like Moses,[4] you might feel a need to remove your shoes to honor the sacredness of the moment and the place it offers you.

This is the reason the language of presence is so frequently on the tongues of mystics. This is how the saints feel in relation to God and how they experience God with them. It is the experience of totality and union in the midst of shattering fragmentation and separateness. It offers fleeting moments of knowing that stand in stark contrast to what our senses tell us so much of the rest of the time.

This is also why presence has such transformational potential. John O'Donohue describes such moments of presence as a sacrament[5]—a visible sign of invisible grace. The source of the grace—or, if you will, the gift—is the Transcendent Presence that is mediated by more immanent forms of presence. Although that source may be invisible (sometimes even beyond belief) and the presence ephemeral, the gifts of the encounter can be readily seen by anyone who has eyes to see.

Pausing
to Ponder

⟐ I have suggested in this chapter that presence has a paradoxical quality to it. Often subtle and easily missed, it can also have great authority and power—sometimes commanding attention and demanding a response. Notice whether you can recall an encounter with someone whose presence carried this sort of authority, an authority that did not come from an imposing personality or authoritarian behavior. How would you describe the quality of the person's presence? If others experience you in this way on at least some occasions, how do you relate to inner authority that, at least occasionally, you seem to carry? How do you understand it?

⟐ Notice whether you have ever experienced, in the presence of another, the hint of a larger presence that was less "his" or "her" presence than something mediated through the person. How do you understand this transcendent dimension of presence?

⟐ If being is presence, what do you know about the way inanimate objects can communicate presence simply through their being? What qualities of presence do your home or other things associated with you communicate? How would this differ from or be similar to whatever presence you might assume you communicate?

⟐ In this chapter, I proposed that the more pure and uncontaminated the presence, the more it transcends the particularities of the person associated with this presence. This may explain the fact that presence feels the same in some fundamental way even when experienced with quite different people. Consider whether your experience supports this.

2

PRESENCE *and* ABSENCE

I have long been nostalgic about presence. Nothing lingers for me like it. Nothing dissolves the sense of distance between me and another person as it does, and nothing makes me feel alive and at one within myself in the way it does. There is, consequently, nothing that I value more highly than experiences of presence and the possibilities of authentic encounter associated with them. I know I am not unique in this. The longing for presence may in fact be the most basic human desire.

Sigmund Freud tells the story of a three-year-old boy crying in a dark room of a home he was visiting one evening. "Auntie," the boy cried, "talk to me! I'm frightened because it is so dark." His aunt answered him from another room: "What good would that do? You can't see me." "That doesn't matter," replied the child. "When you talk, it gets light."[1] This child was not afraid of the dark but of the absence of someone he loved. What he needed to feel secure was presence. We all need the same; knowing presence is the ground of this basic sense of safety for all of us. There are few things more important in life than presence. It is no exaggeration to say that it is essential for human survival and thriving. Think, for example, of the infant's basic need of the presence of an available and attentive caregiver. While infants need to be fed and cared for, it is alarmingly clear that this can be offered in minimalist ways that leave the infant fed but not nurtured. Infants need more than food to thrive. To develop psychologically and spiritually, they also need steady, dependable, loving presence. Seeing ourselves reflected in the loving eyes of someone gazing at us as we gaze at them is the indispensable foundation of psychospiritual health and maturity.

In the absence of this reflective mutuality of the presence of someone who is totally present to them, people go through life somewhat like that little boy in the story told by Freud. They may no longer cry out in the dark, but the distress they experience when confronted with threats of absence can involve almost unimaginable levels of existential panic. Knowing the gift of someone who is fully present to us is, therefore, the foundation of the subsequent ability to tolerate absence.

Tolerating absence is, in essence, trusting presence—even when the one who is present to us is not physically present. Think of the two-year-old gradually loosening his clinging grasp to the leg of his mother as they dance around the house. Slowly, he allows himself longer periods of independent movement, but, at least initially, these bursts of independence are made possible only by periodic rushes back to mother for emotional refueling. Over time he ventures farther away for longer and longer intervals. Initially, he needs his mother to be in sight to keep his anxiety manageable, but soon he is able to tolerate absences that include not just physical separation but his mother being unseen. He has begun to cultivate trust in the stability of presence that is not dependent on sensory confirmation.

Some people fear absence so much that they refuse to allow sufficient space in their togetherness to cultivate this sort of stable knowing of presence. I've known couples that were so clinging in their attachment that they never learned the benefits of space in their relationship—benefits to both the relationship and to each of the partners. The same enmeshment has even more disastrous developmental consequences when it occurs between a parent and a child.

The absence of stable knowing of presence also manifests in the fear of solitude. The capacity to make productive use of solitude presupposes this sort of stable foundation of presence. Solitude isn't simply for those who are shy or introverted. The only way to pass through loneliness to the richness of inner life that develops within regular periods of solitude is to be able to enter that solitude with the full-orbed accompaniment of presence—both presence to oneself and the knowing of the presence of other people and things that mean that one is not, in fact, alone. Solitude does not mean living apart from others; it means never living apart from presence to one's own self.

This is one of the many potential great gifts that can come from a silent retreat. Stripped of the distractions to knowing presence, those who survive the first couple of days of silence invariably begin to awaken to powerful, previously unnoticed forms of presence. I have seen people who believed that rooms had been repainted because the colors were more vivid. Others have asserted with conviction that the kitchen obviously hired a new cook because the food suddenly became so much tastier. When told nothing in the environment had changed, they were incredulous. It is hard to believe that changes of that magnitude and sensory impact are within us—that we are simply becoming aware of things previously unnoticed. Or put in other terms, what is happening is that people are beginning to be present to things that had all along been present to them. They are experiencing an awakening.

◊

If physical and psychological wellbeing are dependent on knowing presence at deep enough levels that we no longer require sensory verification, so too is spiritual health and maturity. In the sixteenth century, St. John of the Cross anticipated the insights of twentieth-century developmental psychology when he described the process of spiritual maturation as involving the same cultivation of trust that comes through the softening of reliance on the senses.[2]

Just as the infant must learn to trust the presence of the caretaker for increasingly lengthening periods of apparent absence, so too must the person who seeks to come to a point of stable knowing of Divine Presence. This is what St. John of the Cross means by the dark night of the senses. Deep knowing emerges only when we release shallow, more superficial knowing. In all aspects of human development, this involves moving beyond what we can know through our senses to what we can know intuitively and subjectively. Just as the stable knowing of the presence of loved ones, even in their physical absence, is characteristic of mature psychological development, the stable knowing of Divine Presence is characteristic of mature spiritual development. This knowing is what Christian mystics describe as union with God, a union based on knowing presence even in the midst of apparent absence.

Spiritual health is no less dependent on knowing loving presence than are physical and psychological health. There is, in fact, no substitute for this encounter with loving presence. No amount of belief or faithfulness in spiritual practices will ever be sufficient to support us on the journey from our false centers in our small egoic selves to our true ground in the Spirit of the One who is our source and destiny.

Perhaps we can think of the core of the human spiritual quest as the pursuit of experiential knowing of the Transcendent. This is the presence that underlies and is mediated through encounters with more immanent expressions of presence. In this journey, we must first deeply know the presence of others and the world if we are to know the Transcendent Presence that lies behind them. This is the truth of the incarnation. God may transcend materiality but has chosen to reveal the God-self in and through physical and material presence. The Word that was God came to us in human form. Logos was enfleshed so that we could know Divine Presence.

Because humans are hardwired for presence, we will always be vulnerable to absence. Even Jesus knew this vulnerability. Nowhere was this more clearly expressed than in his cry of anguish from the cross when he sensed God having forsaken him.[3] Jesus, like us, had to learn that the apparent absence of God is actually a face of the real presence of God. If the stable knowing of the presence of the one he called Father—the presence that so characterized the rest of his life—could be threatened at such a point as this, who are we to expect that we will ever be immune from such vulnerability?

We humans long to be in the presence of those who hold us in love. We also long for the presence of those we love. Many of us also know a longing to experience the presence offered by special places—sacred spaces that ground us, align us, and restore our sense of wellbeing. Mystics long for nothing more than an experiential knowing of the presence of God, and many ordinary people claim occasional moments of such knowing and count them among life's most precious gifts. Many of us know the immense value of belonging within a community, but community is itself presence, not merely an institution or a collection of individuals. In one form or another, we all long for presence because, without the presence of others, we have no way of knowing our own presence or our own being.

Underlying any experience of absence lurks the existential anxiety associated with the separateness of the self from its Source. Describing not only his own sense of separation but also the fundamental root of all human anxiety, the thirteenth-century Sufi mystical poet Rumi invites us to listen to the reed and the tale of separation it tells:

> Ever since they cut me from the reed bed
> my wail has caused men and women to weep. . . .
> Whoever has been parted from its source
> longs to return to that state of union.[4]

Is it any wonder that we rush to fill experiences of absence with presence of some form or another? Quickly, we grasp at available forms of pseudo-presence. Because of their power to mask the experience of absence, these usually take the form of addictions. But while pseudo-intimacy through addictions may distance us from our sense of absence, they eliminate the chance to develop a healthy way of responding to the underlying existential vulnerability. Consequently, they also lessen the chances of transformational engagement with possibilities of presence.

Just as death must be embraced as part of the cycle of life if we are to truly live, the reality of absence must be embraced if we are to experience a stable knowing of presence. Presence can be received only as a gift that comes from openness and trust, not by defensive grasping that seeks to avoid absence.

Without some knowing of the Ground of Being that holds every experience of absence, it is almost impossible to fully live in the now. Absence is defanged with the knowing of Presence. But Presence will always remain an elusive mystery—beyond our control and beyond our exhaustive knowing.

The ebb and flow of presence and absence is the basic rhythm of our lives. Together, they configure our journey through time and space. Yet presence will never be totally absent, and all absence is full of the hidden presence of the Wholly Other. John O'Donohue takes this thought and offers it to us as a blessing:

> May you know that absence is alive with hidden presence, that nothing is ever hidden or forgotten.
> May the absences in your life grow full of eternal echo.
> May you sense around you the secret Elsewhere where the presences that have left you dwell.[5]

⌀ The desire for presence usually emerges out of the experience of absence—something we have all known. Yet the pain of absence hints at a knowing, or at least anticipation of the possibility, of presence. Like the possibility of a just world that none of us has ever experienced, presence hovers as an ideal for which we seem hardwired. What we long for is a presence that will endure absence and equip us to do the same. What do you know of absence and the way that it forms the ground out of which your desire for presence emerges? And what do you know of presence—a presence that helps you endure absence?

⌀ In this chapter, I suggested that tolerating absence is, in essence, trusting presence. Notice how trustworthy (or untrustworthy) presence is for you. Think of the most dependable and trustworthy presence you have ever known. Reflecting on this has the potential to help you understand how you relate to absence. Notice the extent to which your trust in presence goes beyond the senses and is based on deeper knowing. And notice whether this deeper knowing of presence translates into your knowing of Divine Presence.

⌀ I mentioned the insight of St. John of the Cross that deeper knowing of presence emerges only as we release shallower, more superficial forms of knowing. How well does this fit with your experience and your understanding?

⌀ Finally, I also suggested that without some knowing of the Ground of Being that holds every experience of absence, it is almost impossible to fully live in the now. But perhaps you can think of someone who seems remarkably present but who would reject any knowing or even belief in a transcendent Ground of Being. Consider what this might say about the possibility of knowing the Ground of Being without realizing it or describing it in this way.

3

BEING PRESENT

Presence starts with being present. If I am not present myself, other people and things may be present to me, but I will not notice them. So presence must start with me. I must myself be present if I am to know presence of any sort. But this seemingly simple notion of being present—as with so much associated with the concept of presence—masks a rather profound and complex reality. Let me try to unpack that reality and then translate it into practical terms.

Being present has at least two meanings. First, we can understand it to mean being *here*, or being in attendance. I recall as a child answering the daily roll call at the beginning of school every morning when, in response to hearing my name called, the appropriate answer was "Present." This was a shorthand way of saying "I am here." But there is a second meaning to the words "being present." In this sense, to be present is to be in the present moment, or what we might call "the now." The spiritual practice of being present involves both of these understandings. It means to be here *and* now.

In one sense, we are always in the present. Where else could we be? Nothing exists outside the now. Everything we experience is an experience of the moment. Even our memories come to us in the here and now, as do our thoughts about the future. But the question is how much of our consciousness is present in the moment. Clearly our bodies are present, but our minds are usually somewhere quite distant. Dragged along by our thoughts, most of the time our minds are preoccupied with rehearsing the past or anticipating the future.

Consciousness is organized in such a manner that we can be aware of only one thing at a time. I am writing these words as I sit in a doctor's office waiting for an appointment. Suddenly, my awareness shifts from the words I am writing as I notice someone moving in my peripheral vision. Then, for the first time since entering the office, I suddenly become aware of obnoxious background music. Then I hear the voices that surround me. Then I become aware of the passage of time and wonder how much longer I am going to have to wait and if I should now put my computer away. Then I smile as I notice how ironic it is that I am writing a book on presence while so far from awareness of my immediate environment. And now I am back to my thoughts about this chapter. And all this occurred in less than ten seconds.

Even when we try to concentrate on one thing, our stream of consciousness is filled with many other unrelated things. Our thoughts flit around like spawning salmon trying to make their way upriver. But don't be too quick to identify with the salmon. The point of the metaphor of the stream of consciousness is not that we are the salmon or the stream but that we are someone trying to stand in the fast-flowing river, yet being constantly dragged along by the water and things that float down it. If the here and now is where we are trying to stand in that river, this should help us understand why we are so seldom consciously present.

◈

Of all the things that can occupy our awareness and drag us from being in the here and now, none can compete with thoughts in terms of drag potency. For most people most of the time, consciousness is filled with thoughts, and for most of us, our attachment to our thoughts is notoriously robust.

Thinking about the present moment is not the same as being fully in it. Just as maps are not the same as the territory they represent, thoughts about reality are not the same as participating in that reality. All we are in contact with when we are caught up in our thoughts is our thoughts.

Notice, for example, how some people can be with you and appear to be listening to you, but all you can hear is the whir of their minds as they rehearse what they are preparing to say next. They may be making the requisite eye contact that good socialization has taught them to show as a sign of attentiveness, and they may be nodding their heads or smiling at appropriate moments, but clearly they are much more present to their thoughts than to you. And, of course, we all frequently do the same to others.

The startling fact is that thoughts do not exist when you are totally in the present moment. To be fully in the present, we must release our thoughts and get out of our minds. The best way to do this is to return to our senses—and thus to our bodies. Rather than talk about this, let me suggest a little exercise to show you what I mean.

One way to experience being in the present is to attend to your breath. By *attend* I mean be fully present to your breath. To help you do so, you might want to first get comfortable and then, when you are ready, close your eyes. This cuts out visual distractions. Then, to enhance your awareness of your breath, either insert ear plugs (if available) or cover your ears. Now, notice your breath—don't try to change it, just attend to it as fully as you can. Be present to it. Listen to the sound it makes and feel the movement in your chest as you draw each breath in and then release it. As soon as you notice thoughts or any other focus of your attention, simply return to being present to your breath. Don't try to resist thoughts, but don't retain them. Letting go means no grasping and no pushing away. Just release thoughts as you allow yourself to be drawn into presence to your breath. Offer nonjudgmental witness to whatever comes into awareness and then simply release awareness of anything other than your breath, and return to the fullest presence to your breath you can offer.[1]

If you tried this exercise you will likely have noticed that being fully present to your breath is not as easy as it sounds. Hopefully, however, you noticed even brief moments of quieting of thought as you came into presence to your breath. With practice it becomes easier, and the presence that you slide into becomes deeper and fuller. But it does take practice to unlearn the habit of privileging thoughts over awareness.

Presence to the present moment brings a sense of inner stillness and peace. This comes from releasing pressing inner agendas and the stress of obsessive remembering and anxious anticipation. It represents the fruit of the inner alignment that is yours when you do just one thing at a time and you do it with presence.

Being present to another person, God, or the here and now does not require that you first attend to your breath. This was just a way of demonstrating presence. Being present simply involves letting go of all the usual ways we avoid the present moment.

Multitasking is one of the great enemies of presence. In truth, we can be present to only one thing at a time. We may be able to do many things at the same time, but we can be present to only the one thing that is, at that precise moment, our primary focus. Being present simply means being fully where you are. It means intentionally doing only one thing at a time—and investing the fullness of your being and presence in that one thing.

Think, for example, how easily you eat without thinking about the food you're eating. Or notice how often you obsess about things in the past or future rather than fully attend to whatever or whoever is inviting you to engagement in the present moment. Presence starts with being present. There is no alternative to this that does not seriously compromise your own presence.

The best way to practice being present is to practice doing just one thing at a time. When you are eating, just eat. Pay attention to what you're eating. Really experience it. Savor the taste and be sure to notice the texture. Eat slowly and intentionally. Do the same with other things. Just do what you're doing now and nothing else.

What can you expect if you do this? You can expect that, very gradually, the continuous thrashing of salmon in your stream of consciousness will slow down. With practice, it will disappear almost completely. In its place will be a sense of peace, stillness, and contentment. And that says nothing about the potential encounters with others that presence makes possible!

Eckhart Tolle argues that the most important relationship in your life is your relationship with the present moment.[2] I think he is right. If your relationship with the here and now is dysfunctional, that dysfunction will be reflected in every relationship in your life. This is because avoiding the now always involves a minimization or distortion of reality. In the same way, an embrace of the now involves an embrace of reality. Presence always involves an alignment with Life. To choose life is to choose God, and choosing God is choosing life.

Being present involves being attentive because all presence depends on consciousness. In the words of John O'Donohue, "Where there is a depth of awareness, there is a reverence for presence. Where consciousness is dulled, distant, or blind, presence grows faint and vanishes."[3]

The cultivation of awareness is, therefore, central to the clarification and purification of consciousness. But how easily we misunderstand what it means to attend. In the spiritual life, it does not mean to screw up your willpower and tighten your resolve. Spiritual attentiveness is less a matter of concentration than contemplation. It is releasing distractions, preoccupations, and prejudgments and being available for absorption. This is why Simone Weil described unmixed attention as pure prayer.[4]

The key word in this last paragraph is *absorption*. Presence is making one's self available for temporary absorption by someone or something. This is the essence of contemplation. It is quite different than mere thinking, in which the most we can hope to experience is absorption in our own mental processes. Contemplation involves openness to and absorption by something transcendent to the self. In fact, I would go so far as to say that to be present requires some form of contemplation or meditation, as these create space for the inner self to engage with the present moment.

Being present involves an intentional shift from a mode of doing to a mode of being. It is an orientation toward one's experiences in the present moment that is characterized by openness and curiosity. It requires that we make space for that to which we wish to be present.

Presence thrives in places of emptiness, not fullness. Most of the time we are too full to be truly present—too full of our opinions, our preconceptions, our beliefs, our thoughts—too full of ourselves. Spiritual emptiness is nonattachment—particularly to our thoughts and opinions. Presence requires not only an open mind but also an open self.

Being present also requires acceptance. It requires accepting what is, as it is. We cannot be present to anyone or anything in judgment. Offering presence requires at least a temporary suspension of our normal modes of evaluating, judging, and classifying. In fact, it requires a temporary suspension of critical thought. This is why presence has such a relaxed quality to it. But it is not a posture of indifference. Rather, it is characterized by involvement. Acceptance means we receive the present moment and all it presents to us, and engage it as it is. The moment takes priority and is received with hospitality. It is received with a release of agendas and openness to the possibility of us being changed by the encounter.

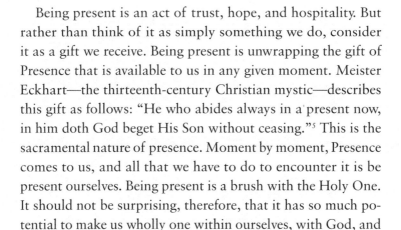

Being present is an act of trust, hope, and hospitality. But rather than think of it as simply something we do, consider it as a gift we receive. Being present is unwrapping the gift of Presence that is available to us in any given moment. Meister Eckhart—the thirteenth-century Christian mystic—describes this gift as follows: "He who abides always in a present now, in him doth God beget His Son without ceasing."[5] This is the sacramental nature of presence. Moment by moment, Presence comes to us, and all that we have to do to encounter it is be present ourselves. Being present is a brush with the Holy One. It should not be surprising, therefore, that it has so much potential to make us wholly one within ourselves, with God, and with all that is.

But presence is not merely a gift we receive. It is a gift we give to everything and everyone around us waiting for us to turn up for potential encounter. It is a gift of mediated Presence.

⌀ Return to the image of presence as trying to stand still in a fast-flowing stream—the stream of consciousness. Notice how you are dragged away from presence by the contents of consciousness as they sweep past you. Now notice the most common contents of your own consciousness (that is, the things you most frequently think about or that most regularly lurk in your awareness) and reflect on your attachment to these things. Remember, your attachments are not only reflected in consciousness but also become the building blocks of your identity, so noticing the contents of consciousness yields important information about the state of your inner self and its unfolding.

⌀ I suggested that thoughts do not exist when you are totally in the present moment, and I offered an exercise of attending to your breath as a way to experience this. If this exercise failed to help you shift from your mind to your body, I'd encourage you to try it again. And again. Be patient with yourself. You have spent a life-time of attachment to thoughts as an unconscious way of avoiding both body awareness and presence so you will have to learn to be gentle with yourself as you attempt to soften this attachment. But do give this exercise a chance to see if it will work for you as well as it has worked for many others.

⌀ Eckhart Tolle suggests that the most important relationship in your life is your relationship with the present moment. Consider how the way you relate to the present moment impacts every other relationship in your life.

⌀ How do you assess your capacity for absorption? If presence is of-fering yourself for availability for temporary absorption by someone or something, what keeps you from offering this availability more regularly?

4

THREE LAWS
of PRESENCE

There is something elusive about presence. If you are attentive, you will often notice it in your peripheral vision, but as soon as you face it directly it seems to disappear. As with many of the most important realities of life, it is harder to know *about* presence than to know it directly. However, of the things I think I know about presence, three in particular stand out as most surprising. All are counterintuitive, yet each has tremendously important implications.

Calling these things "laws" may seem a bit presumptuous, since I did not receive them carved on stone on some mountaintop. Nor are they the fruit of research in anything like the usual sense of the term. I say they are surprising because I can hardly believe that they are true, yet I know they are.

Let me set them out in propositional form before we reflect on them together.

1. Presence to anything starts with presence to self.
2. Presence to anything is constrained by presence to everything.
3. Presence to anything is a threshold to the Transcendent.

Presence is easily faked, but usually poorly. We routinely feign attentiveness—often along with interest—while little of either is actually present. We expect presence to gush forth as from a just-opened faucet, but what flows from that faucet is a very poor substitute for the genuine thing.

Until presence becomes where we live rather than what we occasionally try to generate, our attempts to actually be present will always involve more appearance than reality. Authentic presence is always grounded in authenticity. Because it emerges from our being rather than our doing, it is always grounded in reality. Being present is being real. It is really being in the here and now. Anything else is pretense, not presence.

Although we can intentionally practice presence—and, in fact, this is the only way that it can be cultivated—it can never be reduced to something we do. Until presence is our relatively steady-state mode of being, there will always be a gap between our being and our doing. Because such a gap is so common, we tend to think it is harmless. But while small rifts associated with occasional doing that doesn't flow from the truth of our being might have small consequences, the chasms that often exist between the truth of our being and the lies we live become major fault lines in our souls. No longer aligned with our center, we are forced to live from the periphery of our self. However, cut off from the taproot of our integrity and the truth of our existence, the distance between the truth of our being and the lies of our lives increase as we spiral into an abyss of pretense and nonpresence.

Is it any wonder that in this place of pretense, genuine presence is so impossible to achieve? Until we can be present to ourselves, we can never be fully present to anything. Presence to anything starts with presence to ourselves. We can never hope to know the presence of God or other people until we can be with ourselves in stillness, openness, and attentiveness. Presence to anything starts with presence to the only self through which we can ever know presence—our own.

While presence to anything is built on presence to self, the presence that we will be able to offer ourselves will be constrained by the presence we regularly offer to anything and everything. It is nearly impossible to sustain more presence to anything than we routinely offer to everything.

Remember, presence is an expression of our being, not simply a behavior. It is a soul posture of openness and attentiveness—not something we can turn into a command performance. As we practice presence, we cultivate soul hospitality. We learn to set aside our preoccupations and clear inner space to receive that to which we seek to be present. The hospitality offered by the best hosts is never simply a way of behaving when guests are present. It is a way of being. Presence is a way of being that will characterize our relationships to everything.

The people I have known who have been able to offer me the highest levels of undiluted presence have been, without exception, people who were also unusually aware of and attentive to both their internal and external environments. Their attentiveness did not arise as a result of effort or resolve but as an expression of openness. Their openness was not simply focused on me. While I might be aware of them being profoundly present to me, as I got to know them I could see that this presence was expansive enough that it made room for attentiveness to their emotions, their bodies, their reactions, even their thoughts. It also included awareness of what was going on around them.

Think of how often in the Gospel stories the narrator mentions Jesus noticing something or other. We hear of Jesus seeing heaven torn open and the Spirit of God descending on him, noticing that the crowd he was teaching was hungry, seeing the faith of those who brought the paralyzed man to him on the mat, observing the rich putting their gifts into the temple treasury, and much more. The presence of Jesus never limited his awareness but instead expressed it. Presence is like that.

As the presence we bring to any moment increases, correspondingly the presence we are capable of bringing to every moment also increases. Presence feeds upon itself, just as nonpresence does. Presence to anything grows out of the soul posture of presence to everything.

Before moving to the third law of presence, we need to bring a little more precision to this notion of presence to everything. It is simply not possible for humans to be absolutely present to everything. It is, however, realistic to think of being relatively present to most things most of the time, so let us take that as the ideal. I have known such people, and perhaps you have as well. Let's take a moment, therefore, to consider this sort of presence.

First, let us note what presence to most things most of the time does not mean. Human consciousness operates in such a way that we can be conscious of only one thing at a time. Awareness is more like a spotlight than a floodlight. It can shine on only one thing at a time. Deepening our presence does not change this basic structure of human consciousness.

The big difference between people who are characterized by a high degree of presence and the rest of us is that those who live with presence are not pulled off center by the stream of consciousness that we discussed in the last chapter. They get the same amount of flotsam coming down that stream, and the stream moves as fast for them as it does for the rest of us, but they are much less likely to be pulled off center by it. The reason for their relative immunity to distraction is not a matter of concentration. It doesn't come from screwing up their attention but from loosening their attachment to the contents of consciousness. They have thoughts, and they notice sensations, and they become aware of impulses or memories, but these things do not drag them around because they have learned to detach themselves (at least to some degree) from the content of their consciousness. They observe the things that float down the stream of awareness—ignoring them increases vulnerability to being dragged off center by them—but do not attach to them. They have learned to hold the contents of consciousness lightly and not to equate themselves with the things that float down this private stream of inner experience.

But if it is not a matter of concentration, how do they stay focused on one thing? They do so by allowing themselves to be absorbed by whatever is before them in the present moment. Children have this capacity for absorption, in spades. Adults who tell young children to pay attention are missing the point. Chances are excellent that the child is, in fact, paying attention. What they are paying attention to—or more precisely, what they are absorbed in—is unlikely, however, to be the thing that the adult wants them to focus on. Here, as in so many areas, we need to relearn what we knew as children. We need to relearn the natural human capacity for relating to the world through eyes of awe and wonder. This makes it easy to find whatever we choose to focus on so fascinating that it no longer takes willpower to stay in the present moment. Instead, we can simply allow ourselves to be absorbed by what invites us to presence. Think of the presence of an infant gazing up into the eyes of a loving parent. Notice the sacred stillness in this moment. This is the eternal now. Nothing else exists. Notice also the mutuality of the encounter. Both are fully present to each other. The result is an astounding singularity that is just like the pure tone of a boy soprano hauntingly wafting over the cacophonous static of the rest of life. It is the singularity of presence—being fully present in the here and now and fully absorbed by the moment it eternally offers.

But can it really be that presence to anything is a threshold to the Transcendent? It seems too simple. And, if you have been used to thinking of religious things, places, and rituals as the only way to access the Divine, it probably also sounds too secular.

However, if it is true that, as Sallie McFague puts it, the cosmos is God's body,[1] this means that an encounter with God doesn't require being in a church or doing anything religious. The Eternal Spirit that is the Source of Everything That Is has taken on material form, thereby forever shattering the validity of all distinctions between sacred and secular. The One that is the Ground of All Being is as close to you as your next awareness of anything. All it takes is presence to encounter Presence.

Presence is a thin place. It is a place where we are particularly close to Transcendent realities that are normally beyond our awareness but that always surround us. This is why being present to my breath, or to ocean waves that lap on the shore outside my window, or to the dog who sits at my feet, or to any of the thousands of other things on the edges of my consciousness at the moment can bring me into the transcendent presence that is the Ground of Being. What an astounding truth this is! And you can know it for yourself.

◆

Take a moment to try another little experiment. Think of a piece of music or a work of visual art that speaks to you powerfully and to which you have access. Arrange things so you won't be disturbed and sit with this for at least ten minutes of contemplative presence. Whenever you notice thoughts or become aware of anything else, simply return to soaking in presence to this work of art.

Now, take a few moments to reflect on your experience. Notice if, while you were being present to this work of art, there was any point at which you were swept up and out of your normal mode of listening or looking and drawn beyond yourself and your normal mode of consciousness. Perhaps you can identify a shift from attending to being absorbed—from an active process to a much more passive state. Or possibly you experienced an unusual degree of stillness and inner peace. Maybe you felt more at one within yourself. Perhaps this even included a sense of harmony and alignment—as if you had suddenly been transported to another place and instantly recognized it as a place where all was well and where you belonged. These are just a few of the markers of brushes with the Transcendent that accompany presence to anything or anyone.

The whole world is sacred—as is everything within it and beyond it. Presence is an act of realizing the sacredness of life and of everything that exists. It is an act of awakening. It is a moment in which our eyes are suddenly opened and we see what truly is as it truly is. Such inner alignment and purity of vision is hard to sustain, and so most of us quickly drop back into ordinary awareness and experience. But if we are attentive to it, each act of presence touches us and heals us, restoring something of our lost spiritual perception. Standing at the threshold of the Transcendent, each act of presence offers us a moment of unitive vision—not simply a seeing *of* the oneness of all things but, as Cynthia Bourgeault puts it, seeing *from* the place of oneness that is within us.[2]

◊

Sufis tell a story of a young fish approaching a wise, older fish. "I have often heard about the sea," said the young fish, "but where is it?" The wise old fish answered, "The sea is within you, and you are within it. It is all you have ever known, and yet you do not know it." This, of course, is the human condition. We are in Christ, and Christ is in us, yet we don't recognize this reality. We may believe it, but we don't know it. What's missing is awareness.

Since awareness is presence, awareness of anything opens up the possibility of awareness of everything—as long as we can break through the default state of self-preoccupation. And this is precisely what presence does. It creates space and openness that allow us to be present to more than our usual self-preoccupations. This space allows us to so attend to one thing that we suddenly notice we are no longer thinking of this thing but are, instead, grasped by it and pulled into an altered state of awareness.

Presence to anything opens us to presence to everything. Awareness comes as a byproduct of presence. Rather than having to try to be aware, we simply become aware. We awaken and find ourselves caught up in immediacy. We notice the previously unnoticed, and everything takes on a quality of being more real than we have ever experienced. Reality comes to us more as it truly is than as we see it through the filters of normal consciousness. We see wholes, not just parts, and we may sense something of the harmony of the whole. Even if these moments of seeing are brief and ephemeral, we know that we have touched something that is solid and true. It is true, it is real, because we are seeing through the Transcendent Source and Ground of Everything That Is.

This notion of seeing *through* a self-transcendent perspective—not primarily seeing the self-transcendent reality itself—is very important. In the Hebrew Bible, God told Moses that no one could see the face of God and live.[3] Because presence involves being drawn into the still pool of our own being, some people may occasionally glimpse the Ground of Being. More typically, however, rather than seeing God, we see through the eyes of God. Meister Eckhart puts it this way: "The eye with which I see God is the same eye with which He sees me. Mine eye and God's eye are one eye and one sight and one knowledge and one love."[4] Spiritual awakening is learning to see all things through the eyes of God.

⌀ In this chapter, I talked about how the split between our doing and being leads to our being cut off from the taproot of our integrity and the truth of our existence. In contrast to this, I suggested that presence is alignment with our truth and is, therefore, something that always serves to heal the basic fault lines of our soul. This is why presence to anything must start with presence to self. What do you know about the alignment of your doing and being? What keeps you cut off from the taproot of the truth of your being?

⌀ Ponder the possibility that presence to anything is constrained by our general level of presence to everything and everyone. I suggested that the beginning point in raising one's presence must be presence to self, but that this then should be expected to lead to more presence to other things. The issue is not treating presence as something we do but allowing it to become a way of being. When we do this, almost regardless of where we start practicing presence, we will experience it spreading out and including more of our lives.

⌀ I suspect the most important and, at the same time, practical thing I have offered in this chapter is the possibility that presence to anything can be a threshold to presence to the Transcendent. What do you know of the truth of this? How can you align your life more fully with this truth?

5

CONTEMPLATION *and* PRESENCE

The loving gaze that holds a parent and infant in suspended animation is a gaze of contemplative presence. This is also what you experience when you lose yourself in a piece of music, work of art, or great conversation with a soul friend. It is being in a place of inner stillness and presence that allows you to taste one thing and to know it as it can never otherwise be known. It is allowing yourself to be absorbed, grasped, and fully held by one person, one moment, one sensation, or one fragment of reality—and through this to make contact with the Transcendent Ground of Reality. It is the young Sufi fish, stopping its furious searching for the sea and suddenly knowing that what it seeks it already possesses.

Describing these moments as contemplative draws attention to the close relationship between *contemplation* (or, as it is sometimes called, *meditation*) and presence.[1] Contemplation is learning to access presence. Another way of saying this would be to describe it as the practice of presence. This was the way Brother Lawrence came to understand his inner spiritual work as he engaged in his external physical work in the kitchen of a seventeenth-century Parisian monastery.[2] Chopping food and washing dishes became for him opportunities to practice the presence of God. What he learned was that his intent was more important than his surroundings or behavior. His practice was contemplative not because it was repetitive or monotonous but because of his desire to be present to the One who was present to him.

Contemporary approaches to contemplation are often too mechanical. Some teach that in order to meditate you do special things such as sitting still (perhaps in a special posture), chanting a mantra, or focusing your attention. However, if washing dishes can be contemplative, so too can listening to music, puttering in a garden, sewing, feeding a child, eating, making art, taking a walk, talking to a friend, reading a book, or even writing one. There is nothing specific you have to do, or not do, to contemplate. All that is required is to use the present moment as an opportunity to be present to that moment.

But if contemplation is not primarily a physical matter, neither is it primarily a mental or psychological one. There is no question that it can be a powerful tool to aid relaxation, combat depression or anxiety, change mental processes, and even alter consciousness. But as valuable as these applications are, contemplation is more of a spiritual posture than a psychological technique. It is a posture of openness and attentiveness in inner stillness. It is no coincidence, of course, that this is how I defined presence. How could it be otherwise if contemplation is the practice of presence!

I describe contemplation as a spiritual *posture* because it is so much more than a *practice*. While it must begin as a conscious practice, its real transformational potential emerges when it becomes a way of living. Contemplative living is living with intentional openness and presence.

Anthony de Mello was a Jesuit spiritual master who has much to teach us about contemplative living. His writing is built around stories from the perennial wisdom tradition of the Indian sub-continent that was his heritage and home. Listen to one of the stories he tells:

> To the disciples who wanted to know what sort of meditation he practiced each morning in the garden the master said, "When I look carefully, I see the rose bush in full bloom." "Why would one have to look carefully to see the rose bush?" they asked. "Lest one see not the rose bush," said the master, "but one's preconception of it."[3]

Like most spiritual masters, Jesus certainly included, de Mello tells us that spirituality is about seeing. Contemplation is the way we receive the gift of new eyes that allow us to truly see. It is how we can encounter reality as it truly is, not as we have previously packaged it. Another one of his stories unpacks this thought further.

> A drunk was staggering across a bridge one night when he ran into a friend. The two of them leaned over the bridge and began to chat. "What's that down there?" asked the drunk. "That's the moon," his friend replied. The drunk looked again, shook his head in disbelief and said, "OK, OK, but how the hell did I get way up here."[4]

De Mello is suggesting that we never see reality directly. What we encounter instead can never be more than a pale reflection of it. But since this imperfect reflection is the best we have, it is this that we use when we seek to organize the world by means of words and concepts. The problem is that we confuse these symbols with the reality to which they point.

Another story makes the same point in a slightly different way.

The master always encouraged his disciples to look up at the moon by pointing his finger toward it, but invariably the disciples would look at his finger. "Don't look at my finger," he would exclaim, "look at the moon."[5]

This story tells us that reality lies beyond the finger of our images and concepts. Nowhere is this truer than in relationship to God. The words we use in relation to God are at best fingers pointing toward Ultimate Mystery. The problem is the ease with which we get stuck in the words rather than knowing the reality to which they point. The great danger is thinking we know when we have confused fingers with reality, or maps with the territory they seek to describe.

Contemplation is the way to move from thoughts and concepts to the reality behind them. It fact, it is the only way to do so. Thinking can never help us know the reality words seek to communicate. Only contemplation allows us to encounter this. It cuts through the distance that objective knowing introduces and brings us up close and intimate to what we open ourselves to in stillness and presence. Contemplation can, therefore, be understood not simply as a way of being but as a way of knowing.

Some things can be known by thought, but the most important things can be known only contemplatively. Think, for example, of knowing love. Thoughts about love are a poor substitute for knowing love, but if you allow yourself to be present to it, you can know love more deeply than would ever be possible by means of the mind.

We can, therefore, also describe presence as contemplative knowing. It is the altered state of consciousness in which we allow ourselves to know subjectively rather than objectively. In presence, we allow ourselves to be absorbed by that to which we seek to be present. Rather than "getting" it, we allow it to get us. This is not the same as focusing on it, and it certainly is not the same as thinking about it. In fact, both focus and thoughts are incompatible with contemplation because they impede absorption. They are mental mechanisms of manipulating reality that keep us in control and interfere with our ability to genuinely make ourselves available for encounter.

In Christian spirituality, this is the core of the important distinction between what is often called discursive meditation and contemplation—or between what I call "pondering" prayer and contemplative prayer.[6] Thinking about God is not the same as being with God in stillness. Contemplative prayer is wordless presence to the One who is present to us. Words, thoughts, and intentional focus can all have great value in prayer, but they all are obstacles to contemplative knowing, which is more a gift of being than the result of doing.

◆

Truly transformational knowledge is always personal, never merely objective. It involves knowing *of*, not merely knowing *about*. Transformational knowing is always relational. It grows out of a relationship with the object that is known—whether this is God, one's self, another person, or something impersonal.

We cannot truly know something or someone from a distance. It requires encounter. Words can be the vehicle of this encounter, or they can be—and often are—a barrier to it. Even though I have never met Anthony de Mello, I have encountered him. I know very little about him, but I know him in a deeper way than merely knowing about him. Our only point of contact has been his words, but because my engagement with him has been contemplative, it has allowed those words access to deep places within me.

Alternately, I think of people with whom I have spent quite a bit of time in shared physical presence and about whom I know a great deal but of whom, I would have to say, I know very little. Sadly, I have never truly met them.

Presence is the most personal form of knowing possible for humans. Rather than objectifying that to which we seek to attend, we encounter it—subjectively and personally. Near the end of the Christian creation story, we read that Adam knew Eve and they became one flesh. Now that's personal knowing! Sexual union is intimate, loving encounter. Describing this as *knowing* reminds us of the essential features of all knowing through presence. It is participative, personal, and deeply intimate. Contemplation is learning how to access this state of participatory, personal, and deeply intimate presence and knowing.

Pausing
to Ponder

⌀ Reread and ponder the opening paragraph of this chapter. Notice what you know of contemplative presence and how that fits with the way I describe such presence there. What words would you use to characterize the knowing that flows from contemplative presence?

⌀ Some people feel theologically defensive when Anthony de Mello speaks of the limitations of words and thoughts as symbols of the reality to which they point. What is your response to de Mello on this matter?

⌀ What do you know about how contemplation can be a means of knowing reality, not merely knowing about it? What do you know contemplatively, and how does this compare with things that you have come to know in other ways?

⌀ How do you respond to my suggestion that presence is the most personal and intimate form of knowing available to humans? If this is true, what difference might it make to the presence you seek to offer yourself, others, or God? Take a moment and reflect on the presence you offer the person with whom you are most intimate, and consider if your presence could further deepen this intimacy.

6

DISCERNING PRESENCE

We noted earlier that since being is presence, everything that has being has presence. This means that everything that exists has presence. Presence is not, therefore, limited to those who are present in the here and now but is communicated by everybody and everything all the time.

Much deeper than personality and more stable than mood or ego state, presence is the signature of our souls. Yet it will often be missed and, if noticed, will be ignored or misread. It takes trust in intuitive knowing to discern. It also requires being comfortable in the subjective and intersubjective spheres of relationships. To those who demand objective, scientific knowing, presence will forever remain unknown.

Animals are often much better at discerning presence than humans. Undoubtedly, this is because they are more aligned with their being—their basic nature. Not confused by false ways of being, they are able to recognize the soul signature of other animals and humans.

Dogs, for example, are keenly aware of the energy of other dogs and seem equally attuned to the same in humans. It is not unusual, therefore, for pet dogs to be highly sensitive to the emotional states of their owners—often more sensitive than other humans. Other animals also show the same skill in reading the soul signature of humans. Wolves are reportedly attracted by the scent of fear, while horses evidently become nonresponsive to someone who is anxious. Perhaps this sensitivity to the soul signature of humans was at play in the fabled response of animals of all kinds to St. Francis. If birds did indeed gather to listen to his sermons, perhaps it had more to do with his presence than with the content of his preaching!

There is no question that some humans are better able to read the presence of others than most of us. I think, for example, of how those who are most keenly aware of their vulnerability will avoid people in whom they sense danger, instead seeking to be with people whom they intuitively recognize as being more free from hostility, judgment, or other peril.[1] I recall, for example, my gay friends who tell me how easily they can identify homophobes, and I think of those who have been sexually abused and their ability to sense sexual danger.

I also remember a young blind albino girl I worked with in intensive psychotherapy for over a decade. As a child she had been sexually and physically abused on a number of occasions and at the hands of a variety of foster parents and other adults. Then, when she lost her sight at age ten, her blindness—particularly when combined with her albinism—made her an easy mark for anyone seeking a highly vulnerable young girl. This soon led to yet new forms of abuse. However, it was not her woundedness that most astounded me but her resilience. Although she was often powerless to protect herself, she showed amazing ability to sense safety or danger in people, and she used this as a powerful way of taking as good care of herself as she was capable. What she displayed was a keen ability to read presence. It and Braille may have been all she could read, but her blindness did not in any way interfere with her ability to see the soul signature of those in her immediate environment.

Most of us miss the presence of others because we are too pre-occupied with observing, listening, and confirming preconceptions. In short, we are lost in our own mental processes. Sigmund Freud gave invaluable advice to psychoanalytic therapists when he warned of the danger of listening for what we think we already know. Instead of listening for facts or details, he suggested listening with evenly hovering, free-floating attention.[2] In such listening, you attend to what gets you, not what you can grasp or you think you have already grasped. It involves what psycho-analyst Theodor Reik later described as listening with the third ear—that is, attending to the depths of your own subjectivity to notice the way the subjectivity of the other person impacts you.

While psychoanalytic listening is not the same as contempla-tive knowing through presence, they are closely related. This tells us that if we wish to better discern presence, we need to shift our attention—beyond the data we receive through the physical senses—to what we can sense more intuitively and subjectively. This does not require that we abandon our minds—something that, even if possible, would be far from desirable. Critical pro-cessing of the subjective impressions that come to us intuitively is always important. Opening the channel of our intuition merely offers the mind more data. It allows us to listen with a third ear and see with a third eye.

Everyone has the capacity for such expanded knowing. Think, for example, of a time when you felt uncomfortable in the presence of someone. If you reflect further on this, perhaps you might have sensed that you were being subtly manipulated. Or maybe you sensed the presence of deceit that made someone feel untrustworthy. At the level of physical sensory data, there might have been nothing that you could identify to warrant such feelings. Yet you might have found that your sense of discomfort cannot be easily dismissed. Of course, you may have been misreading your experience. Possibly it told you more about yourself than the other person. But equally possible, perhaps it was giving you information about this person and telling you something that emerged in your depths in response to his or her presence.

The best psychotherapists, spiritual directors, and counselors are highly attuned to this sort of information. This does not mean that their reading of their intuitions is flawless, but it suggests that it is possible to read to some degree or another the soul signature that others carry wherever they go and express through their presence.

Any trustworthy reading of the presence of others will arise within the context of a deep and trustworthy knowing of one's self. Only when you know yourself well can you be trustworthy in noticing an inner reaction and discerning that it is not typical of you in such a situation. Of course, it is still tremendously easy to be wrong in this judgment—unconsciously projecting onto others that which is unacceptable within us. But, with practice informed by the feedback of a spiritual director, psychotherapist, or skilled soul friend, it is possible to learn to recognize when your subjective experience is being impacted by the presence— not merely the behavior—of someone you are with.

Presence is always read on the screen of one's subjectivity. It requires, therefore, attunement to your own subjectivity. If you don't know yourself, you will miss it. Even if you know yourself to some degree but tend to ignore your inner experience, you will never notice the subtle ripples that cross your soul when you are being impacted by the presence of someone.

Discernment of presence requires much more than knowing information about yourself. It requires a high degree of awareness of the subtle movements within your depths. Sometimes these will appear in your body—perhaps a sudden tension or sense of heaviness—or possibly just the opposite, a welcome sense of lightness and expansiveness. At other times, awareness will surface in your spirit—perhaps a surge or depletion of your energy or some fluctuation within your sense of buoyancy, openness, or trust. In each case, the knowing is what I would call soul-knowing—that is, knowing that comes from attentiveness to the place between spirit and body, which is the soul.[3]

As we noted earlier, sometimes the presence of a person is so commanding that it cannot be ignored. It pulls you into presence and demands your awareness. This is most true of the luminous presence of someone who is aligned and singular within his or her being and through whom, therefore, Presence itself radiates with particular clarity. I have given some examples of this earlier, but the example that would immediately spring to mind for most Christians is unquestionably Jesus. However, even those encountering Jesus in person often failed to recognize the Christ. So, if people could fail to notice the most luminous presence to ever walk this earth, clearly luminosity can be missed.

But if it is possible to miss Perfect Presence, how much more so is this the case when the luminosity is clouded. This is the most common face of presence. It is one that characterizes most of us and the one, therefore, that we most regularly encounter in others. Sometimes the clouding itself produces such a strong reaction in those who encounter it that it is hard to ignore. Much more often, however, when we encounter a clouded presence, all we notice is behavior or personality.

Over the next two chapters, we will examine these various faces of presence, starting with the most common clouded forms, since these are the ones we most regularly encounter, and then turning to luminous presence.

Pausing *to Ponder*

⌀ What do you know of your soul signature? As you read further, you will have a chance to reflect more on your presence, but initial reflection at this point should help you deepen your self-understanding as we move forward.

⌀ In this chapter, I suggested that we tend to miss the presence of others because we are too occupied with observing and listening when we interact with them. I also suggested that we tend to hear only what we think we already know, and therefore we engage with others through our preconceptions of them—often doing little more than seeking confirmation of these preconceptions. To what extent do you think that these things limit your own discernment of the presence of others?

⌀ How attuned are you to any response to other people that might register beyond consciousness somewhere in the depths of your subjectivity? Since presence is always read on the screen of our subjectivity, what limits your attentiveness to this dimension of interpersonal encounter? What value could you see in being more aware of the unconscious impact others might be having on you or you might be having on others?

7

CLOUDED PRESENCE

Personality is seldom clouded. Think of your circle of acquaintances. You don't have to be a psychologist to be able to identify salient personality traits for each of them. You might identify one as gentle, another as shy, yet others as ambitious, cynical, playful, depressive, intuitive, anxious, serious, intelligent, manipulative, provocative, sarcastic, seductive, witty, or a broad range of other things. Each of the people you are thinking about are more than this single trait, but it might be the thing that is most stably characteristic of them. In some cases, you might have trouble finding the correct word or words to describe it, but some feature of personality is usually dominant and persistent enough that it serves as an identifying feature of the person. This, however, is not their presence. These words simply describe a salient dimension of their personality.

The presence that shadows us all is deeper than our personality and yet often more difficult to discern. It is with us in every interaction and will influence others one way or another—even though most people will be unaware of it. It lurks and lingers but is easily ignored or missed. The major reason for this is that it is so often clouded.

Clouded presence is hard to read. The waters of the soul are opaque and restless. You may sense that someone's surface presentation does not tell the whole story, but the nature of that deeper story will be as unclear as the person's presence. Let us look at three common forms of clouded presence and see if we can learn something about how each serves as an obstruction to luminous being.

The most difficult presence to read is what I would call a *confused presence*. This is unfortunate because the clouding can make it hard to realize why such a person so often really upsets you. People who display confused presence are hiding behind a persona. They are not aware of hiding behind anything, but if they are even moderately self-reflective, they will have some awareness of the nature of their public faces. They will, however, think of it simply as who they are and will be totally unaware of how much it creates the confused presence they radiate like an aura.

The core of the confusion arises from the fact that such people have very limited self-knowledge and are dishonest about what they do know. Their heavy investment in impression management is built on a foundation of self-deception. They see themselves as they want others to see them, but they have little awareness of just how strangling this persona is on the truth of their being.

I think of a woman I know who delivers her persona like a polished stage performance. Most of those who work with her recognize her professionalism and high degree of competence, and with a mixture of envy and respect, they are quite aware of how she always somehow manages to deliver a very high quality product. Most would also be aware of her efforts to be helpful when she feels she has something to contribute to a team or individual working on a project. They might also note that she works hard at being seen to be a team player rather than a lone ranger and appears not to need either the credit for the results or control over the process. However, what makes this a persona rather than simply a person with a lot of talent who is eager to help is what she can't acknowledge about herself and what the skilled delivery of her role often makes others slow to recognize. This is why so many people are confused by her way of being and unclear about why they so resent her eagerness to be helpful.

What she is unwilling to acknowledge about herself is her lust for power and need for control. Both are common and socially acceptable in her workplace, but for reasons of her personal psychology, she is unable to admit them to herself or others. She must, therefore, exercise control in covert ways, and she does this with consummate skill. But it is this obscuring of her motivation and her need to be seen as the persona she thinks she is that leaves people confused. She, in turn, is puzzled by the ambivalence she is smart enough to be able to recognize many of her coworkers feel in relation to her.

You don't have to be perfect to have a clear and unambiguous presence. But pretense will always confuse it. Pretense compromises our grounding in reality. It also produces the complexity that complicates knowing how to relate to such a person and the confusion you feel when engaged with her or him. This confusion is clarified only when you understand the ulterior motivations and needs that are opaque to the individual. Because the person who is hiding behind a persona believes that he or she *is* that public face, the presence that is their soul signature is experienced as mixed, clouded, and confused.

A more common cause of a clouded presence is preoccupation. In our age of multitasking, social media, and virtual relationships, *preoccupied presence* is what most of us tend to offer others. It shouldn't be a surprise, therefore, that it is what we usually receive in return. A preoccupied presence is cluttered and fragmented. There is no singularity and no stillness. Our being isn't aligned with the present moment and what we seek to be present to. Instead, it is scattered among the things that preoccupy us as we circle around them in ever-deepening ruts. Instead of being present to what is beyond our self, we are simply present to the tangled conversations that run in a fixed loop in our head.

The agendas we bring to our engagement with people also cloud our presence. The British psychoanalyst, Wilfred Bion, understood this and advised that psychoanalytic therapists learn to set aside memory, desire, understanding, and even caring in order to be able to be truly present to the patient.[1] He recognized that desires always drag us from the present moment, even seemingly normal and benevolent desires such as remembering and understanding what we hear or making our presence helpful in some way for the other. These things, he was convinced, always cloud our presence and decrease the probability of full-orbed encounter. I am convinced he was right.

When I say that preoccupation clouds presence, I mean that—much as in what we saw happening in the case of hiding behind a persona—preoccupation robs our being of the singularity and alignment that otherwise give it luminosity. Because most of us are so familiar with preoccupation, we are not usually confused by it. We simply accept whatever presence we are offered, no matter how diluted it is. Like birds living in major metropolitan areas that lose their natural song and begin to mimic the sounds of the city, we get accustomed to clouded presence. It's no wonder we are so startled when we encounter someone who is truly present to us!

◆

The third major style of clouded presence is *ambivalent presence*. This refers not to ambivalence about presence but to presence that is characterized by ambivalence. People who communicate an ambivalent form of clouded presence are conflicted in ways that those with confused or preoccupied forms of presence aren't. Encountering them, you feel yourself awash in a sea of uncertainty and movement. You feel as if you are being pulled in different directions or are trying to navigate strong countercurrents. What you are sensing is the person's inner experience. Internal conflicts are at the core of the lack of inner stillness, and even though the person may think he or she has successfully resolved or masked these conflicts, it is extremely difficult to set them aside when one seeks to offer intentional presence.

All sorts of inner conflicts can create a soul-aura of ambivalence. I think of someone I know who is highly conflicted around her desire to please and to be authentic. I also think of another who is conflicted around perceived needs for safety and a longing for freedom and authenticity. But I have also experienced the same form of presence in people who are conflicted over their desires—often fearing the strength of their anger or sexuality.

For many years, I was conflicted about the amount of influence I seemed to possess. I recall being at a leadership camp when I was fifteen and being confronted by a counselor who told me that he sensed that I was ambivalent about leadership. Not sure I even knew what ambivalence meant, I immediately denied his assertion. But as time passed and I continued to think about his puzzling observation, I had to acknowledge his perceptiveness. Increasingly, I became aware that I was uncomfortable with my personal power and influence. I wasn't sure I always wanted to be the default leader in groups in which I found myself. As I began to write and speak, it was with a keen sense that, while I didn't want followers, my influence was clearly increasing. A friend kept teasing me that my gift was wasted since I was such a reluctant guru. Over time, I was able to affirm a dimension of my being and calling that I had been unable to accept, and, out of this, my ambivalence about being a person of influence decreased. But I have no question that the presence I offered during earlier decades was colored by this approach-avoidance drama playing itself out on my inner stage.

The fact is that others can sense in our presence things that we do not yet know. The astute and wise person with us in these encounters has an incredible opportunity to nudge deeper knowing of self and resolution of the conflicts that are contaminating our presence.

◆

Clouded presence is not reducible to either personality or psychopathology. The clouding and the confusion it causes in others is a result of the gap between being and doing, a misalignment with one's soul. The more clouded the presence, the more the gap grows into a chasm. When we encounter such a person, we run the risk of falling into this chasm. It is what Jesus spoke of when he compared hypocritical religious authorities to the blind leading the blind—the danger, he said, is that both will fall into a pit.[2]

The confusion associated with clouded personalities is caused by the fact that, although the pit is papered over by the false self, something in the person's presence suggests misalignment within the depths. Something warns of an inner abyss that holds potential danger for others. The greater the person's sphere of influence, the greater the danger for all involved.

The sobering fact is that reality counts. There are consequences to living with fictions that mask our inner realities. To some extent or another, this is true of all of us. None of us is perfectly aligned with the truth of our being. All of us live with falsity, but the magnitude of the gap between inner reality and outer appearance will always be an indication of the magnitude of the clouding of presence. And even if that posed absolutely no hazard to anyone else, it is a symptom of soul pathology that should not be ignored.

The biblical image for clouded presence is seeing through a dark glass.[3] Face-to-face is the biblical language for presence. It is the opposite of seeing through a dark glass. Rather than meeting a distorted reflection of the truth of the other, face-to-face encounters shower us in light, intimacy, and immediacy. This is what we long for—to look into another's face and see our gaze returned. Although we are much more accustomed to clouded presence than the luminosity of direct encounter, our souls always know the difference.

⌀ Clouded presence reflects a clouded soul. The truth of our being is easily compromised by our way of living in relation to it, and the result is that we are out of alignment. We so easily become accustomed to the gaps between the realities of our inner world and the outer life we live, that we, typically, no longer are aware of the dysfunction they reveal. But others will sense it at a deep level of their being when they engage with us. Clouded presence is a symptom that should call our attention to the state of our souls. Ponder what most captured your attention in this chapter. Consider whether the things that made you think of others may, at least in part, be a reflection of something unacknowledged but true of you.

⌀ We all have a persona. We differ only in the extent of our investment in creating ourselves in the image we wish others to have of us. When this investment is high, so too is the clouding of our presence. How do you assess the extent of your own investment in image maintenance? Heavy investment in image is one of the core components of a false self and is tremendously common as a source of clouded presence.

⌀ What preoccupations, agendas, or inner conflicts tend to most cloud the presence you bring to interpersonal engagements?

8

LUMINOUS PRESENCE

Luminous presence is sufficiently rare that we are blessed if we have ever encountered it with recognition. Many may not be aware of any such experiences. This is because, when we meet people, we often fail to encounter the presence they carry as their soul signature because we are not ourselves present. We may, therefore, have *met* luminous presence but not *encountered* it.

Yet, as was the case for clouded presence, luminous presence is not something that is either present or not. So think for a moment of the person who was most present to you and whose personality and preoccupations were the least clouding of this presence, and you have at least a glimpse of the luminous nature of the gift these people carry and share with all who are present to them.

Like a warm, bright light, luminous presence shines through a person in a relatively unclouded manner so that you notice it, not the person. It is like looking at several things in a field of vision and having your attention captured by only one of them. Their presence is the one in focus and most commanding of your attention. Yet, at any time, you are aware that you could shift your attention to other things that are also present. One of these is the uniqueness of these people—their personalities. Yet the presence they communicate is both separate from this and in many ways more striking. This is why I say it is not so much "their presence" as a presence that they mediate.

It is not just limited experience, however, that makes it hard to describe luminous presence. Words are also woefully inadequate. As with anything that is truly transcendent, presence is mysterious and ineffable. It defies analysis and explanation, even easy definition. This is why it so often evokes wonder. In luminous presence, we encounter the purity of simple being. Being is simple—not complex, but singular and pure. Life is complex. Personality is complex. Mind, self, relationships, and experience are all complex, but being has about it a singularity that marks it as pure.

To be pure is to be natural—to possess the singularity of life in the Garden of Eden and to know that you are at home within your Source. It is to be aligned with the truth of your being—no pretense and no falsity. Think of the purity of a young child's actions and ways of being. Young children may lack maturity, but they do not lack authenticity and alignment. Being and doing are seamlessly interwoven.

Being is the spring, and doing is the stream. In the alignment of simple being, the water that flows from the spring down the stream is pure and free of contaminants. But when we no longer go to the source to collect our water, the stream will draw its water from a variety of other places, and what flows down the stream is no longer pure. This disconnection of being and doing represents a misalignment of our souls that clouds our presence to ourselves and others.

The purity of simple being is luminous because all being emanates from the One who is Being. In Christ, we live and move and have our being,[1] but Luke, who is believed to have been the author of these words, was not the first person to realize this. The teaching that humans have their origins in God's being goes right back to the creation story where we encounter the powerful metaphorical imagery of God's breath vitalizing the dust of the earth and leaving us unalterably connected to our origin.[2] Nothing exists that does not have its origins in God. God's presence holds and makes possible all other forms of presence. If God were not present, all presence of everything else in existence would instantly cease.

This means that human presence is fundamentally related to being human. Luminous presence shows us what it means to be fully human—created in the image of Presence. What makes us truly human is our capacity for presence and encounter.

The astounding nature of being human is seen most clearly in presence and love. The two are intimately related. The "I-Thou" relationship is one of love in that I set aside my individuality to honor the uniqueness of the other. Presence is putting my whole self at the disposal of the one I encounter. It is a way of listening in love, and it is a way of being in alignment with Being itself.

Every act of presence—no matter how imperfectly luminous—brings a healing touch to the depths of our souls and increases our capacity for presence and encounter. It connects us to our being and involves a brush with the Ground of Being.

One way of thinking about the sort of clear and commanding presence that Jesus displayed—when he was teaching in the synagogue and people were amazed by what the Gospels describe as his authority[3]—is to think about it as the outflow of the simple being that was the spring at the center of his being. All his doing clearly emerged from his being in union with the Father. His identity, words, and actions all flowed from this source, and all reflected his absolutely perfect alignment with the truth of his being. This is the simplicity and purity of being that expresses itself in Jesus as the personification of Luminous Presence.

Is it any wonder that simply to encounter Jesus was to encounter the Ground and Source of Being? Is it any wonder that many were deeply threatened by his presence? It carried a challenge to all who encountered him to live with the same purity of being that can come only from alignment with the Ground of Being.

The more we are lost in the self that we think we want to be or the self that we have created as the expression of our own complicated desires, the more we will find the call of Jesus to follow him to be a profound threat. Many deal with this threat by simply ignoring Jesus. We Christians often adopt a more sophisticated way of managing the threat he represents. We tame Jesus, reducing him to a sentimental object of belief or attachment but failing to be touched in our depths by the purity of being that comes to us in his presence. We worship him rather than follow him.

The One who is absolute purity of being is described in Scripture as a consuming fire.[4] The purity of God is an awesome thing—something that those who truly encounter God will always experience with fear and trembling. No wonder we feel such a strong need to domesticate God! Rather than be purified, we desperately seek to protect our small, fragmented ego-selves from the holiness and purity of the One. Religion is our way of doing this. It is our idea, not God's. God's invitation is to join the One in simplicity of being that involves union in Presence.

Even though the idea of purity of simple being may be attractive to a part of us that longs for the rest it represents, simple being will always be a profound threat to the complexity we have protectively wrapped ourselves within. Like the Gadarene demoniac who encountered Jesus and who named himself Legion because "we are many,"[5] we too are all many. And the many will always feel threatened by encounter with the presence of the One.

However, if simple being is a purging fire, it is also the warm hearth at the center of a welcoming homecoming. Our existence is the outflowing life of the Ground of Being. Our presence is a reflection of the Presence behind all luminous presence. The luminosity of simple being is our origin and destiny. It is alignment with the truth of our being.

As we cross the threshold and enter into an encounter with luminous presence, we feel the inviting warmth of that hearth and experience a deep sense of letting go. For at least a moment, we release everything that stands between us and simple being. If we listen carefully we might even hear a sigh emerge from the depths of our soul as it enters the rest of this sacred place.

Simple being is a deep sigh of relief that comes from letting go of pretense. It is also the sigh that comes from releasing a heavy burden that results from creating and managing the false selves that are substitute centers for the truth of our being. It is the sigh of release as we exchange complexity for simplicity. It is the sigh of release as we let go of preoccupations, inordinate attachments, and disordered passions. Things in the depths of our beings get aligned when we let go of these things. Even if we pick them up again and try to put them back into place, their places in our souls will be different because we have consented to a first release of them, even if just for a moment. That's the way presence heals and transforms us in our depths.

Notice that as we reflect on the light and warmth of luminous presence, we have not focused as much on the person who offers us the encounter with Presence as on our experience in the encounter. Remember, presence is not as much a characteristic of the person as it is what she or he mediates. The person recedes into the background, and we are simply aware that we are in a very thin place.

But if luminous presence is not really about the person who mediates it, we might wonder why it is so rare. The answer is the vulnerability of simple being. Stripped of all the things we use to protect it, the self is insubstantial and very fragile. Remember the Christian creation story; we are but creatures of dust and breath. But dust and breath both lack substance, and this leads to our sense of vulnerability. To protect ourselves from the vulnerability, we wrap our fragile selves in layers of things that are designed to give them more substance—things such as possessions, accomplishments, and reputations.

But the problem this creates is that we then identify with these layers of protective wrap, not with the fragile, naked self that is our simple being. Rather than taking our identity from the "I AM" who is the ground of our being, we take it from such ephemeral things as what we do and what we have. Paradoxically, therefore, the things in which we wrap our selves actually make them less substantial rather than more. While they give us the illusion of substance, they weigh us down and, wrapped far too tightly around our naked self, they cut us off from the supply of vitality that would otherwise come from simple being. Thus, we lose the lightness of being that is our birthright. We lose our connection to the Ground of Being that is our center.

While I have been focusing on luminous presence in humans, let us not forget that since everything has presence, the presence of animals, trees, and rocks can also all be powerfully luminous—as can the presence communicated through works of art and other human constructions. Some who have never known such presence from a human may know it quite well through nonhuman encounters.

Here, too, it seems to me that the luminosity of such moments of presence arises from simple being—from the purity of being that exists in something that has no option but to be what it truly is. Aesthetics, personal history, and spiritual sensitivity also are involved in allowing one person to experience the powerful and clear presence of a tree while another merely sees the tree. But the simplicity of being on the part of the tree is the basis of the luminosity of presence it reveals.

Martin Buber's distinction between relating to an "It" versus a "Thou" is also highly relevant to our notice of luminous presence in both human and nonhuman meetings.[6] In fact, we should probably see it as the central dynamic of spiritual sensitivity. Buber reminds us that every "It" can become a "Thou" or, perhaps better, already is a "Thou" that we can learn to recognize.

Simple being involves a restoration, but it is never simply an achievement. We lose the simplicity and alignment of our being when we lose our center and adopt false identities. Our identity will always shape our presence—and our sensitivity to the presence of others. And for most of us, our identity is quite distant from simple being.

Our identity is forged from our attachments. Simple being comes from attachment to our source—to the "I AM" in whom our existence is held. But because of the vulnerability of simple being, we trade "I am" for "I do" and "I have." Then we become our attachments. Simple being and luminous presence come from returning to our center and allowing our identity to be grounded in our being, not in our doing and having.

⊘ What do you know of the simplicity of being as opposed to the complexity of living? What would allow you to know more of the purity of simple being? How could you live out of a place of deeper alignment with the truth of your being?

⊘ Jesus never allowed himself to be distracted by the complexities of his self or his life. He kept his eye singly on his being in the Father. Consider how the complexities and false strands of your identity keep you from knowing the joy of simple being.

⊘ "I am," "I have," and "I do" are the three major potential foundations for an identity. Notice the extent to which your own identity is built around what you have or do and how this might keep you from being grounded in the "I AM" who is the Ground of Being.

⊘ What things help you meet others as a "Thou" rather than an "It"? To the extent to which you have been successful in making this shift, how does it affect your knowing of their presence? What do you know about engaging inanimate objects or nonhuman living things as a "Thou"? What potential might this hold for meeting other humans as a "Thou?"

9

PRESENCE
and INFLUENCE

Recently, a young woman approached me, asking if I had any advice for her about writing a book. I asked why she wanted to write a book, and she said that she had always wanted to be a person of influence and had decided that becoming an author was the best way to accomplish this goal.

Everyone today seems to want to be a leader. Social media offer ways to collect followers and measure personal influence, and leadership gurus are full of advice about how to become such a person. They tell us that to be the sort of person others will follow, one must—among other things—possess charisma and confidence; be persuasive, flexible, and resourceful; and have good communication skills and judgment.

I have been interested to note, however, that some leadership experts are beginning to question the reduction of leadership effectiveness to traits and skills.[1] Like the young woman who asked me for advice about becoming an author, they recognize that the essence of leadership is influence. But they suggest that the source of influence lies much deeper than in skills and personality. They suggest it lies in presence.

But how does presence work as a source of influence? To this point, I have described it as our soul signature and suggested that the luminosity of this signature is a function of our alignment with the simple truth of our being. I believe this is true, but I also recognize that it does not go very far toward helping us understand the powerful field of influence that is associated with even relatively luminous presence. Taking a closer look at the relationship between presence and consciousness will, I think, help us do that.

*

Consciousness is the state of awareness of our internal and external environment. At the present moment, for example, you might be conscious of the act of reading, of the presence of related thoughts, perhaps also of tangential paths down which these thoughts lead you. These are all internal environment phenomena, but at the same time and displaying themselves on the same screen, sounds, smells, or a large number of other bits of information are coming to you from your external environment. Consciousness draws from both these sources and provides us with the evidence that we are alive.

Normal consciousness refers to the customary form this takes when we are awake. Although it is a very limited form of consciousness, normal consciousness is the default state in which we spend most of our life. It is the background noise that typically fills our awareness, the buzz of static that is made up of thoughts, worries, anticipations, plans, tasks, sensations, and perceptions. The contents of our thoughts reflect the level of the development of our consciousness. For example, when our primary identifications and attachments are related to our bodies, our identity will be based on one form or another of what we could call a body-self, and consciousness will be filled with thoughts related to our body, our image, our possessions. Higher levels of consciousness development are organized around our mind, soul, and spirit, and all have associated with them a characteristic normal state of consciousness.[2]

Altered states of consciousness do not refer to these levels of consciousness development but to temporary alterations of whatever is our state of normal consciousness. Sleep, for example, is an altered state of consciousness because it involves a distinctly different experience than normal waking consciousness. Similarly, psychoactive drugs also alter consciousness, as does meditation or contemplation.

Presence is an altered state of consciousness. It involves what Eckhart Tolle describes as a "still and alert attention,"[3] which is quite different from the frenetic mental activity associated with normal consciousness. The state of consciousness in presence involves a curious combination of absorption and openness—neither of these being typical of normal consciousness. It is this combination of absorption and openness that allows us to be in the here and now much more than is usually true for most of us.

◊

Presence is a very special altered state of consciousness in that each act of presence involves an awakening. Awakening yanks us from the intermediate zone of thoughts, judgments, opinions, beliefs, and classification of experience, and places us firmly in a more direct encounter with that which truly is. Instantly, it lifts us out of our preoccupations and well-worn ruts of inner dialogue and brings us into the now. Entering presence is walking through a doorway as we leave a small room and suddenly finding ourselves in the vastness of a vibrant, endlessly expansive universe.

In presence, we awaken at least momentarily to ourselves, to others, and to the world. Although we tend to quickly fall back into our habitual somnambulistic fog, each awakening is a threshold for the transformation of consciousness. In presence, we touch our own being and face the possibilities of being touched by the being of others. In presence, we inhabit our bodies and souls more fully, and because of this, we become more alive. John O'Donohue describes this state of belonging to our soul as the thing that keeps presence aflame.[4] It also gives presence its vibrancy, immediacy, vitality, and potency—and all of that grows out of the special state of consciousness that presence occupies.

The power of presence comes from the fact that deeply inhabiting one's body and soul invites others to do the same. This is why we feel more alive when in the presence of someone who offers us presence. Presence invites presence. It is an awakening that invites others to awaken. It is an altered state of consciousness that invites others to also fully inhabit their bodies and souls.

Being present is infinitely more powerful than anything one can do or say. Although it may give rise to words and actions, these will always be empty and will lack potency without presence. But when they are embedded in presence, they come with an authority that is hard to deny.

Think, for example, of Jesus calling his disciples to follow him. The Gospels describe this as occurring within a very brief encounter.[5] Words were few. What got the disciples attention that day as they were going about their business mending their nets was not a forceful argument but a forceful presence. Only this was powerful enough to cause them to leave everything behind and follow Jesus.

At its best, leadership is influence through presence. Persons of influence who are present to themselves can then be present to others—both individuals and large groups. The potency of Jesus's teaching and the fact that others recognized him as carrying astounding authority came from his presence and the way it bore witness to the truth of his being. That—not rhetoric, manipulation, hypnosis, or any other source of influence—is the basis of the most powerful natural authority and source of influence we will ever encounter.

Presence doesn't offer narrowband influence. It doesn't simply inspire others to work harder or accomplish more. That is motivational influence. That's workplace management pep talk. Presence operates quite differently. Paradoxically, it invites us to become more than we are by returning to the truth of who and what we already are. Deeper than an invitation to doing, it is an invitation to being that holds the potential to become the source of all our doing.

Influence can be for good or for bad. We have already noticed the lurking danger of clouded presence. Misalignment with the truth of one's being is soul pathology that is toxic for both one's self and others. The greater a person's sphere of influence, the greater the danger for others, and nowhere is this danger greater than when it involves religious and spiritual leaders. Recall the warning of Jesus about false prophets who are wolves in sheep's clothing.[6] The true nature of such people will always be eventually recognized, but the damage to those who are within their sphere of influence will be great.

Sometimes a clouded presence can become dark, and the nature of the influence even more malignant and destructive.

The name we give this is *evil*. This is the word we feel compelled to use when people engage in the deliberate and systematic destruction of ethnic, racial, religious, or national groups of people. Think, for example, of Hitler, Stalin, Idi Amin, and Pol Pot. It is also language that springs to our lips when we hear of mass murders, the exploitation and abuse of children, and the torture or senseless killing of animals.

When we think of evil, we tend to think of persons, not the patterns of influence that nurtured their hatred and encouraged their actions. Behind every individual who commits heinous acts is the dark presence of someone who is using his or her power of influence to lead others toward the intentional destruction of life. The influencer may not even know the one being influenced, but you can be sure that those being influenced are keenly aware of the presence of the one who models the hatred they seek to emulate. Listen to the rant of those who hit the front pages of our newspapers with atrocities they have committed, and you will always be led back to the dark presences that were the sources of influence that shaped their development. Presence is neutral. It will always be powerful, but the nature of its influence depends on the person that carries the presence. It is not influence but presence that should be cultivated. Influence comes with presence as a bonus. Unfortunately, however, those who seek influence are often precisely those whose influence is most often untrustworthy. Their lust for power makes them dangerous. The danger is not in their presence but in the misalignment of their beings. Their natural talents and cultivated skills may allow them to succeed in building the power base they seek, but what they display is never luminous presence—no matter how much glitter is associated with their way of being in the world.

⊘ If leadership is truly influence, it is interesting to note how powerful
leadership is often exerted by people without any formal leadership
role. Think about examples of this in your experience. Notice the
quality of the presence of these informal leaders, and consider how
it either supports or suggests needed modifications to the understanding of presence and influence I have offered in this chapter.

⊘ Think of your own experiences of presence—being present yourself
and being in the presence of someone who was luminously present to you—and consider the alteration of your normal state of
consciousness that this experience seemed to involve. What words
would you use to describe the alteration?

⊘ When has presence served for you as an awakening? What happened and what, if any, continuing effect on you did this awakening have?

⊘ In this chapter, I suggested that the power of presence comes
from the fact that deeply inhabiting one's own body and soul
invites others to do the same. Notice how well your experience of
presence aligns with this and consider how you understand the
power of presence.

⊘ Think about your encounters with people you might describe as
dangerous—possibly even evil. How would you describe their presence and the source of their influence?

10

ENCOUNTER *and* PRESENCE

It is now time to shift our attention from *presence* to *encounter*. While my primary focus to this point has been on presence, you may have noticed that I have been unable to avoid talking about encounter. The reason is that it is impossible to separate them. There can be no presence without an encounter and no encounter without presence.

Even the act of being present to yourself involves an encounter with your presence. The same is true when you are present to a sunset, a person, your pet, or God. In each case, you encounter something or someone. If you do not encounter anything or anyone, either you are not present or your expectations about what form that encounter should take are getting in the way of it actually happening.

Presence is never, therefore, strictly solitary. It always involves a relationship. More particularly, it always involves a relationship between an "I" and a "Thou." Presence involves honoring the sacredness of whatever or whomever you seek to be present to. Even presence to ourselves demands this same honoring. Anything approached as an "It" will never be encountered. But anything approached with reverence for its sacredness has the potential to become an encounter.

Every "It" can become a "Thou." And you hold the key to this transformation. That key is the way you engage it. Engage with honor and its otherness will be revealed to you through an encounter with a "Thou." But engage with anything less than this and you simply meet an "It." It all depends on you.

True presence means being the presence of a "Thou." This is the mode of being in which we encounter the sacred that is the hidden treasure in everything and everyone. We don't have to look for it. The sacred reveals itself to us when we approach it as a "Thou" seeking to encounter another "Thou."

There is no reason to suspect that Moses set out looking for the sacred on the day when he suddenly encountered a burning bush that was not being consumed.[1] He was simply going about his daily work, tending the sheep of his father-in-law, but the fact that he noticed not only that the bush was burning but also that it was not being consumed tells us that he was attentive to the transcendent. He was attentive to the extraordinary in the ordinary and to sacred presence.

Anyone might have noticed a bush on fire and passed by, but Moses was so sufficiently present in the moment that he noticed that the bush was not being consumed. This led him to come closer, and as he did, he encountered not merely a mystery but the Sacred Presence that lay behind it—the Presence that revealed itself as the "I AM." Moses encountered the "I AM" because he approached the bush as the presence of a "Thou." And his encounter with God confirmed that both he and God were also a "Thou."

Only in presence is it possible to know presence. Only in bringing the presence of a "Thou" to a meeting can the other reveal itself as a "Thou." And only in bringing the presence of a "Thou" to a meeting can that engagement become an encounter with the Eternal Thou—the Wholly Other that lies behind all encounters and every other Thou. This is the great mystery and the great truth that is revealed in the story of Moses and the burning bush. Every encounter with an "other" can be an encounter with the Wholly Other. For in each particular "Thou," we encounter the Eternal Thou.

What does it mean to treat yourself as a "Thou"? And how does this shape the potential encounter when you seek to be present to yourself? The nature of an act is determined by the motivation out of which it arises. This is the source of its meaning. We recognize this when we speak of doing the right thing for the wrong reason. An act of apparent love that does not arise from a heart of love is not love.

An act is made sacred by the intentions that shape it. Being present can be nothing more than a psychological technique, useful, for example, in treating anxiety, depression, or a range of other issues. But the same action of being present can also be prayer. Prayer is not a behavior but an intention—an intention of openness in faith to God who is both beyond and within one's self. Presence as prayer involves a sacred offering. It involves offering myself in the moment, to the moment, and to the possibility of an encounter with what that moment holds.

Sacred acts are free of the instrumentality that characterizes much of human action. It is not true prayer when we expect to get something from the act of openness. Genuine openness in presence means setting aside our hopes and expectations about what we might gain from being present. It is stepping outside our usual mode of doing so that we may return to being.

Being present to one's self, or simply being present in the moment, can be a sacred act when it is offered with this openness. Openness means, of course, that we must be prepared to be open to whatever the moment may hold. We can never, for example, be open to God without being open to our own selves. Nor can we be truly open to our selves without being open to the God who inhabits the depths of our selves. There are no closets or drawers in openness. Nothing can stay hidden in a heart that is genuinely open. This is why prayer is honesty and honesty is prayer. All that is required to make presence a sacred act of prayer is to be as open as you can be in that moment. That will always be enough.

All encounters require that at least two parties turn up in presence. That is not difficult for bushes, buildings, and bridges. In fact, nonpresence is not even an option for inanimate objects whose blueprint of existence is the elegance of simple being. Nor is nonpresence an option for God since, as the Ground of Being, God is the source of all presence and all being. Only humans seem to face the possibility of compromised presence through clouding or darkening of their soul and its signature.

Encountering a "Thou" requires seeing past projections, prejudices, and preconceptions. These are the things that characterize so much of our interpersonal engagements. We think we know someone and expect a meeting to simply confirm what we already know, but only when we are prepared to meet the other in their sacred uniqueness do we have any chance of an authentic encounter with them. Only then do we have any chance of an encounter with the Wholly Other that is in them.

This requires what I would call holy curiosity. Our curiosity about others is often abysmally limited, and where it exists it is often more an expression of voyeurism than the desire to meet others in their sacred uniqueness. Holy curiosity cannot exist until we can believe that there is much more to the other person than what we think we already know of them. Beyond this, we also must genuinely *want* to get to know them in their otherness in a way that will shatter our preconceptions. Familiarity tends to obscure the presence of the stranger in those with whom we are most intimate. Only when we learn to show hospitality to the stranger that is part of everyone we meet can we discover that in this act we are showing hospitality to the Wholly Other who is within each of us. Remember the words of Jesus—our actions and attitudes toward others are actions and attitudes toward him.[2]

To say that every human being is an "other" is to say that each person possesses a uniqueness that can never be reduced by our knowing or contained by our preconceptions. But often we feel that we don't even have to know someone personally to know everything that is worth knowing about him or her. This is the core of prejudice, and this is what is in operation every time we make a judgment based on things such as appearance, ethnicity, education, culture, religion, or social class and assume that this tells us everything that is important to know about a person.

No one can ever exhaustively know another human being. This is both the great mystery and great loneliness of our individuality. While we can never fully know others, it is their "otherness" that has the capacity to enrich not just our knowing of them but also our experience of the world and ourselves. These are but a few of the many great gifts of authentic encounter.

◆

Presence is sometimes misperceived as self-preoccupation. Nothing could be further from the truth. Because it is always relational, presence always orients us to something beyond the small ego-self of normal consciousness. The possibilities of encounter all arise from this orientation to that which is beyond—beyond our control, even beyond our grasp, beyond our imagining, and beyond what can be met within our normal consciousness.

Every act of presence is an act of love because every "I-Thou" encounter involves setting aside the ego-self to meet the other. When we meet in presence, we cease to be strangers. Encounter involves at least temporary intimacy, and such loving engagement always has a humanizing effect on all participants. Love nurtures our being. It makes us more fully and deeply human.

Presence is the doorway to encounter and, as we shall see, all encounters are potentially transformational. This is because encounter always involves a brush with the transcendent. It involves contact with something beyond the parties directly involved in the encounter—something transcendent to them. Presence always points toward Ultimate Presence. This sacramental nature of encounter is, I believe, the key to its transformational potential. And because presence is the necessary precondition of encounter, even a moment of presence is a threshold to awakening, authentic being, and more complete becoming.

Sadly, we usually miss the potential encounter with Ultimate Presence that awaits us in these brushes with the transcendent. Preoccupations and distractions keep us self-encapsulated. This limits presence and makes genuine encounters tragically rare. We may meet people, but typically we encounter only our opinions and judgments about them. Their otherness, or what Martin Buber called their "Thou-ness," remains hidden because of our failure to distinguish between an "It" and a "Thou." Consequently, both parties are deprived of the opportunity for any authentic encounter. All real living may, as Buber asserted, lie in meeting, but this requires that we be prepared to no longer settle for "I-It" transactions and be ready for the potentially transformational encounter of "Thous."

Before ending this chapter, I would like to return to a comment I made near its beginning. I referred to the fact that our expectations of an encounter can easily serve as a barrier to experiencing it. While it is natural to have expectations, the problem is that they serve as a subtle mechanism of control. Although we might not be conscious of it, encounters present us with both a threat and a curiosity. The threat lies in the fact that the other has the power to challenge our way of being. Simply by virtue of living from another center of meaning and approaching the world from another vantage point, the other is a threat to our basic life posture and a challenge, therefore, to our spirituality.

Even when we allow ourselves to respond to holy curiosity by moving toward engagement, we tend to want to manage encounters. One of the ways we do this is by means of anticipation and expectation. Anticipation usually takes the form of mentally rehearsing how we might approach and engage the other. Our expectations flow out of this, being built around the outcomes we assume we might reasonably anticipate. But orchestrated engagements are not authentic encounters. Even if the script is loose and the expectations relatively open, they alert us to the fact that we are approaching the engagement with our hands still on the controls.

The richest gifts of encounter come to us when we are able to take our hands completely off the controls and receive the "other" in whatever form the encounter takes. Only in the vulnerability that this involves can we encounter not just the "other" but also the Wholly Other.

Pausing
to Ponder

- Reflect for a moment on the difference between encounter and a simple meeting. Think of someone you met (perhaps even briefly and only on a single occasion) who impacted you deeply and positively by the very nature of his or her being. Notice how different such a meeting is from the more typical meeting of someone socially or professionally. Notice what was different in you as well as what was different about the person you encountered.

- I suggested that both presence and encounter should be understood as always existing in relationship to a Transcendent horizon. Consider the possibility that presence may be a response to Ultimate Presence, and that encounter with another might always in some mysterious way involve an encounter, even if beyond awareness, with the Wholly Other. If this is true, what implications would it have for you?

- Notice and reflect on the way some of your engagements with people are "I-It" meetings while others may be closer to the ideal of an "I-Thou" meeting. What keeps you from more regular presence as a "Thou"?

- Consider whether you have had any encounters with inanimate objects that would qualify as "I-Thou" meetings. If so, what was different in you in such encounters as opposed to the times when you simply engage them as "Its"? Think of an occasion when you received the Eucharist or Communion and notice whether your encounter with the bread or wine involved your bringing the presence of a "Thou" to the meeting. How could you more regularly encounter the sacraments of everyday life in the flow of your typical day?

11

DIALOGUE *as* ENCOUNTER

Few things seem easier and yet are, in fact, more challenging than dialogue. We think dialogue is easy because we confuse it with things like discussion, debate, conversation, or the simple exchange of opinions or information. But dialogue is profoundly different from each of these things—as different as prayer is from talk about God. A good discussion may include sharing opinions and knowledge, but it involves much less risk and requires lower levels of trust than dialogue. Debates—which are about winning or losing, not about discovery and exploration—are, of course, even more distant from genuine dialogue.

Dialogue is exploration and discovery through conversational engagement. It is shared inquiry that is designed to increase awareness, understanding, and insight. It is the place of meeting that we have been calling encounter. Dialogue holds the promise of providing participants with access to a larger pool of meaning and understanding than they had before the encounter. It holds the possibility of changing not just opinions, perspectives, and understandings, but us. It involves two or more people talking with each other for no other purpose than to deeply meet each other. In dialogue, each says to the other, "This is how I experience the world. Tell me how you experience it." Dialogue is, therefore, the form of sharing of one's self in which we witness the truest turning toward and engagement with another person. It is the archetypal "I-Thou" encounter.

Dialogue yields personal knowledge that is quite different from the impersonal knowledge that is produced by "I-It" engagements. Personal knowledge is "knowledge *of*," whereas impersonal knowledge is "knowledge *about*." Personal knowledge is more intimate than impersonal knowledge and, consequently, much more transformational.

Dialogue demands reciprocity and always involves synergy. In this regard, we can think of it as collaborative creativity. Something new is always created or discovered in a dialogical encounter. Often, this is an expanded and enriched understanding of some aspect of reality, but when it involves genuinely meeting another person and encountering something of the truth of her or his being, it always brings with it an expanded understanding of self and the world as well as new possibilities for living and being.

In genuine dialogue, the "other" becomes present, not merely in one's imagination or feelings, but in the depths of one's being. This is a remarkable thing, and if you have never experienced it, you will have trouble making any sense of this assertion. However, if you have experienced it, you will know immediately what I am speaking of. But this presence of the other in the depths of your being requires that each person first be a person in his or her own right. It also requires that we come to dialogue fully inhabiting our own traditions since we never truly encounter others within the context of their traditions if we do not speak from the deep ground of our own.

Over the last several decades, I have been blessed to be able to participate in extended periods of dialogue with people of other spiritual traditions—particularly Taoists, Buddhists, Muslims, Jews, and the indigenous people of Canada. When I first began to pursue these dialogical encounters, I was so curious about the people I was meeting that I didn't want to dilute the conversation with much of my own story. I wanted to get to know them and their stories and failed to realize that I could come to know their stories only within the context of sharing my own. It takes at least two to dance the dance of dialogue, and both must be prepared to turn up as people deeply situated within, and willing to share, their own traditions. Only then can we meet others within their traditions.

I recall a good friend of mine who spent several years in Southeast Asia studying and practicing meditation. As he was ending this time and preparing to return to Canada, he asked his teacher what he needed to do as the next step in his journey. His teacher's answer was that he needed to engage more deeply with his Christian roots. My friend was shocked by this and replied that he had never been more than a nominal Christian. Displaying more wisdom than I suspect most Christians in the same situation would show, the teacher told him that his Christian roots were much deeper than he realized, and that if he wished to truly make the things he had learned in the East his own, he now had to complete the circle by re-engaging the cultural and religious roots of his being. [1]

Sadly, dialogue can be used to avoid deeply living one's own spiritual tradition. I sometimes encounter people in interfaith and intercultural dialogue who are lurking on the edges of real encounter because they are dabbling in dialogue without deeply living their own culture and tradition. But if we are prepared to deeply live our own traditions rather than be dilettantes moving among the world's wisdom traditions and picking up bits and pieces that we happen to like, there is no alternative to the wise advice of my friend's teacher.

Curiosity and respectful listening are not enough for dialogue. Dialogue demands a deep enough meeting that we actually become participants in the life of the other. What was between two people is now within each of us. This is the mystery of dialogue, a mystery that lies right at the core of its transformational potential.

The key to the transformational nature of dialogical encounter is how it makes changes in the self at the boundary of self and non-self. Often this takes the form of a blurring of the boundary of "me" or "us" versus "them." When I am able to meet you as a "Thou," dialogue will always soften this boundary between me and everyone else—a boundary that we establish to keep us safe from the unconsciously feared threat of the "other."

But the price of admission to genuine dialogue is high, and there are no scalpers to sell you admission tickets that are cheaper than the going price. That price is the willingness to be changed by the experience. Authentic dialogue demands consent to the possibility of being changed by the encounter. Beyond this, it also demands that we be prepared to hold our understandings of truth with humility. Thich Nhat Hanh suggests that for true dialogue to occur, "We have to appreciate that truth can be received from outside of—not only within—our own group. If we do not believe that, entering into dialogue would be a waste of time."[2]

Once again, it comes down to openness. No debater approaches a debate seeking to meet the opponent in openness, prepared to experience a broadening of his or her understanding and ways of seeing the issues being debated. Rather than looking for openness, all you seek in a debate is an opening to forcefully make your point and make the position of your opponent look as ridiculous as possible. Communication is similarly not burdened by a need for openness. Communication requires being clear about what you already know and transmitting this information in as organized a manner as possible. This might involve attentiveness to the audience but does not usually include openness to the possibility that the engagement might alter your understanding of the things you are trying to communicate.

Dialogue both demands and offers much more than this. In relation to discussion and debate, dialogue is more about exploring than proving, more about discovery than making points. In dialogue, knowledge is employed as a gift, while in debate it is used as a weapon. But the true gift in dialogue is not simply one's knowledge but one's self. This is why dialogue can occur only within a context of trust and respect. We may need some degree of safety to share our opinions and knowledge, but it is even more essential that the environment be free of threat if we are to feel safe enough to share our deepest selves in dialogue.

Dialogue is always a win-win encounter. It strives for the engagement of two or more persons in ways that honors both their separateness and their connectedness. It also supports the development of each participant's ever-deepening understandings of self, others, and the issues being explored. When dialogue is pressed into the service of more specific tasks, such as solving problems or effecting change, it immediately loses its potency as an opportunity for the free and mutual sharing of selves. This is particularly true when one of the participants in the dialogue has a goal of doing something with or to the other, even something as benevolent as promoting their growth. However, when dialogue is entered with mutuality, goals of growth and development are quite compatible with the non-manipulative ideal of the interpersonal engagement I am calling dialogue.

◊

Dialogue is one of the most intimate forms of soul engagement we can experience with another person, but it is precisely for this reason that we fear it. For many people, the possibility of being changed by the other is simply a deal breaker. For others, the confrontation with alternate ways of being in the world is simply too threatening.

Many people are so mistrustful of other beliefs and spiritualities and so certain of their own grasp on truth that they are incapable of any forms of interpersonal engagement other than argument or proselytization. They fear encountering another person in the mystery of his or her life because they unconsciously recognize that doing so might bring them into contact with the mystery of their own. Meeting someone in dialogue always involves at least a temporary suspension of our presuppositions about ourselves and the world. This means it always involves a degree of vulnerability to truth.

A lack of genuinely knowing one's self or a fear of doing so also serve as major barriers to dialogue. What I have to give to others in dialogue will always be directly proportional to the depth of my knowing of myself. If I do not know myself, the only self I have to offer in dialogue will be a false self. And false selves are only comfortable with other false selves. True and most authentic ways of being emerge with difficulty under conditions of a meeting with a false self. But to the extent that I am genuinely and deeply my true self, others who meet me are afforded an opportunity to also be their true selves.

Both a lack of courage and a fear of intimacy also block genuine dialogue. It takes courage to respond to the invitation to share one's self with another person. If I am afraid of genuinely meeting another self, I will prefer a conversational form that makes fewer demands on its participants. Genuine dialogue is an intimate encounter. It is not for those who lack the courage to honestly engage with another.

Finally, dialogue is also impaired by a need for control. One can control interviews and conversations, but one must surrender to genuine dialogue. Much like moving into a flowing stream of water, one must enter dialogue ready to let go and be carried along on a journey.

We can create opportunities for dialogue, and we can participate in it, but we don't actually create dialogue, nor can we ever control it. If we must control where a conversation or relationship goes, we will never be ready for genuine dialogue. If, however, we can temporarily relinquish our need to control others and ourselves, dialogue offers a unique opportunity for an enlargement of the self of all participants.

Chances are good that many of you reading this book will be interested in presence and encounter from a professional, not merely a personal, perspective. Perhaps you are a counselor, psychotherapist, or spiritual director and have already been thinking about the implications of what we have been talking about for your work with those whom you accompany in relationships of soul care or spiritual companionship. Dialogue should—and can—form the very core of these interactions, and when it does, it can change them from helping relationships to transformational encounters. However, genuine dialogue is far from normative in professional relationships, and there are a number of good reasons this is the case.

Professionalization of work has brought with it many good things. Standards of practice and performance, expectations of expertise, a framework of accountability, codes of ethics, and lifelong continuing education and training are but a few of these. But professionalism has also brought with it an easy slide into playing a role rather than turning up for personal encounter. Too easily, professional relationships become "I-It" relationships. This does not need to be the case. There is nothing incompatible between being professional and meeting another as a "Thou." Nor does dialogue require a denial of the fact that in professional relationships, the roles of the two parties are not the same.

The real question is whether or not we turn up in a professional context with presence and openness to dialogue. The alternative to this is to hide behind our roles—bringing our care and expertise but not our true selves. This always involves objectification and emphasizes technique, but when we are willing to meet the other as a "Thou," and open to the possibility that, in meeting them in the midst of their experience and ideas, we may change, the dialogue we share can be a transformational encounter. If we cannot offer this, the relationship may involve expertise and empathy, but it will never be an encounter worthy of being called dialogue. And it will never hold the possibilities of transformation for all involved that an authentic dialogical encounter holds.

Pausing to Ponder

⌀ Think about conversational engagements that you have had with others that come closest to some of the ideals of dialogue presented in this chapter. How would you describe what you experienced in these encounters? What effect did the encounters have on you?

⌀ Notice the tension that is involved in fully inhabiting your own tradition while at the same time meeting other persons in theirs. Think of people who you sense do this with more ease, and reflect on what might make this more possible for them.

⌀ Read and reflect on the encounter of Jesus and the Samaritan woman as recorded in John 4:4–42. Consider whether this meeting can help you better understand the possibilities and practice of dialogue. Notice any ways in which you might want to restate the nature or ideals of dialogue in the light of this encounter.

⌀ Finally, take a few moments to reflect on your own barriers to dialogue. Resist the temptation to reduce your own dialogical encounters to the absence of time or presence of interesting people and instead notice your own resistance to it.

12

TRANSFORMATIONAL ENCOUNTERS

The modern world offers abundant opportunities for connections. People can now be in touch with their friends almost continuously. If this sounds like an exaggeration, you haven't spent enough time with teenagers recently!

Social media provide ways of engaging with friends that are important and highly worthwhile. They are also spiritually significant. They remind us that connections lie right at the heart of spirituality—connections with friends, others, one's own depths, God, and the earth. However, the connections that are fostered by social media seldom involve either presence or encounter, and consequently, while they may be significant, they are highly unlikely to be genuinely transformational.

I am convinced that there can be no transformation apart from presence and encounter. No one is transformed simply by experience—regardless of whether the experience is winning the lottery, a close brush with death, or falling in or out of love. If transformation happens in relation to life events, it is not because of the experience but because of how the person responds to the experience.

Presence is the way you open yourself to the possibility of transformation. Dramatic experiences can change the circumstances of your life but do not alter consciousness and identity unless you engage that experience with deep presence and welcome the encounter that it offers. It might, like Saul's experience on the Damascus Road, not immediately be the sort of experience you would naturally welcome, but if you choose to embrace it with openness, it has the potential to leave you forever changed.

One of the surprising things about a transformational encounter is how brief it can be given the magnitude of the changes that can result. Dreams seldom last longer than fifteen to twenty minutes, but history gives us abundant examples how such nocturnal encounters can change a life. In the fourth century, Christ appeared to Constantine the Great, emperor of the Roman Empire, in a dream that changed him and the history of both the West and of Christianity. Following this encounter, Constantine converted to Christianity and subsequently made Christianity the religion of the empire. Similarly, the angel Gabriel appeared to Mohammed in a dream, telling him to leave Medina and go to Mecca—an act that Islamic historians credit with the establishment of Islam as a world, not merely a tribal, religion.

The Bible presents us with many accounts of equally significant transformations of a life through a dream encounter—transformations that subsequently changed other individuals, communities, and even the world. To mention just one of these, recall the beginning of the transformation of the Hebrew patriarch, Jacob, as it is described in Genesis 28:12–17. Jacob had just stolen the birthright from his brother Esau through deceit and treachery when, learning of his brother's plan to kill him in revenge, he fled to his mother's relatives. At the end of the first day of travel, he stopped for the night and, after falling asleep with his head on a stone, dreamed of a ladder stretching between earth and heaven with the angels of God going up and down. Above it stood the Lord who told Jacob that he would be with him and would watch over him wherever he went, ultimately bringing him back to the land he was fleeing and giving it to his descendants.

Jacob's stubbornness meant that he required a second nocturnal encounter before his metamorphosis was solidly in place. On the night of his return to his brother and his land, we read in Genesis 32:21–34 of a vision in which he wrestled with God, refusing to release God until God blessed him once again. He got his blessing, but he also got a new name (Israel) and a new identity. Even more important, as a result of these two nocturnal encounters, the world got Judaism, which ultimately was to be the ground out of which Christianity would arise.

Brief transformational encounters, however, are not limited to dreams. They can be as simple and direct as getting into conversation with someone sitting next to you on an airplane or waiting in line at a concert—a connection that quickly turns into rich dialogue and an encounter that you might remember for the rest of your life. I am blessed to have had a number of these encounters, and perhaps you have as well.

Not surprisingly, Jesus had many of them. Think, for example, of his encounters with Nicodemus (John 3), the woman at the well (John 4), the man born blind (John 9), Martha (John 11), Zacchaeus (Luke 19), or the rich young ruler (Luke 18). Jesus's life was full of relatively brief engagements with people, engagements they would remember for the rest of their lives. Encounters can be like that.

◊

One New Testament encounter has always struck me particularly powerfully. Perhaps this is because I can so easily see myself within the small group of people that were together on this day. Here is how I imagine it through the lens of Luke's version of the story:

It has been a week from hell—well, not quite a week even though it feels like an eternity. Everything we believed in and worked for suddenly imploded. Instead of waking up from a bad dream, it is more like descending into one and slowly discovering that the apparent dream is, in fact, the new reality. But it is a reality that makes us question everything that has happened in our lives during the last three years.

The first sign that things were heading in a bad direction was supper on Thursday. As we were eating, Jesus shocked us by saying that one of us was going to betray him. Hardly able to believe our ears, we asked with fear and trepidation which one of us would do this. Turning to Judas, Jesus then told him to do what he had to do quickly. We were all stunned. Could Jesus really mean what he said? Perhaps we had misunderstood him. Judas, however, seemed to understand because immediately he got up and left the room. The rest of us simply sat in shock. But quickly things got even worse. Jesus said that soon he would be going away and that we would all be scattered, leaving him alone. What on earth was he talking about? None of us understood, but neither did we want clarification. For myself, I simply wanted out of that room. The tension and confusion were suffocating.

After supper, we followed Jesus to a garden where we had often met. After Jesus prayed there, we saw Judas enter with a group of soldiers and religious officials. Now I knew we were all in trouble! Within a few moments, Jesus was arrested, bound, and taken away. And, just as Jesus had predicted, we all scattered.

The next morning, I heard from the others that Jesus had been taken to the chief priest for questioning and was now being seen by Herod. Several of us went to Herod's palace to see what was happening, but just as we arrived, we saw that Jesus was being led away. A crowd was following him, and the word was he was being taken to Golgotha for crucifixion. In a daze, I stumbled along behind the crowd, not sure I wanted to be there but unable to do anything but follow the procession.

The rumors were right. A few hours later, Jesus was dead on a cross. I saw some of the other disciples, but mostly we stood in shocked silence. What was there to say? What was there to do? Later, we followed—still at a safe distance—and watched as he was buried. It was a dark, dark Friday! I'd call it Black Friday.

Sunday was just as confusing. Cleopas and I decided to go to Emmaus since there was no longer any reason to stay in Jerusalem. So we set out that morning, talking about what had happened, telling and retelling what we had seen and how all our hopes and dreams had suddenly crashed and burned. As we walked, we met a stranger who asked us why we were so upset. We told him, and he listened with interest, but then he shocked us by asking us why we were so slow to believe everything that the prophets had foretold. He then went on to tie all the pieces together, explaining how everything that had happened to Jesus had been predicted in the Scriptures. Remarkably, we had never seen the connection. And so, as we approached Emmaus and as the stranger was about to head off on his own, we begged him to stay with us and share a meal so we could talk further.

He agreed to stay with us for dinner. While we were eating the most remarkable thing happened. The stranger took the bread in his hands, gave thanks to God, broke it, and gave it to us. As he did this, we instantly recognized that the stranger was none other than Jesus! Then, just as suddenly, he disappeared. We look around the inn, but he was gone. But it almost didn't matter because we had awakened from that devastating dream. We still had a thousand questions about what was going on and what it all meant, but one thing was different. Hope had replaced despair. We could see. We knew Black Friday wasn't the end we felt it had been. Perhaps it was just the beginning! Perhaps it would actually turn out to be Good Friday![1]

This seems to me to be worthy of being called a transformational encounter. Without this and the disciple's other post-resurrection meetings with Christ, they would never have had the courage or conviction necessary to tell their story in a way that would change the course of human history. But this encounter contains the seed of all authentic encounters and helps us see the reason an encounter—any encounter—holds such transformational potential.

Ultimately, the presence that transforms is not ours, nor is it that of the other person we encounter. The transformational presence is that of the One who is with us in the encounter. Remember the words of Jesus: Where two or three of you are gathered together in me, there am I in your midst.[2] With the disciples, we usually fail to recognize the presence of Christ in our midst, but it is his presence that vitalizes the encounter.

Encounter always invites awakening. With the disciples on the road to Emmaus, we also need enlightenment. We need to see the One who is present with us, in us, and among us. We could call this awakening, but we could also call it enlightenment or even conversion.

Because the presence of the Christ is usually hidden, transformational encounters do not necessarily involve recognition of his presence. Remarkably, this failure to recognize Christ's presence does not eliminate the transformational possibilities of encounter. His presence is what counts, and he is present in every encounter, recognized or not.

Let me share a story that illustrates the transformational nature of even an anonymous encounter with Presence. When

I first met her, Judith introduced herself as a Jew who was on the road to becoming a Christian.[3] This caught my attention, and I asked her to tell me more. She said she had been raised in a secular Jewish home that was devoid of religious interests or sympathies. Her parents had taught her that spirituality was merely softheaded religion and was, therefore, the enemy of the hardheaded realism that was necessary to be successful in life. But, she said, despite both this family culture and her parents' present alarm at her apparent softheadedness, nothing was more important to her than following her spiritual quest.

The catalyst for these changes had been, in her words, an encounter with an atheistic Jewish psychoanalyst. She said that it wasn't what he said or did that had influenced her but the impact of who he was and his way of being. She felt that it was this that called her to focus on her own being and this was what slowly led to the emergence of her spiritual interests. These, in turn, led to her work with the mystics, her discovery of Teresa of Ávila, and her subsequent interest in Christianity. And all this from dialogue with an atheistic Jewish psychoanalyst!

Much to the chagrin of her family, Judith did eventually convert to Christianity. But the point of her awakening was her encounter with someone whose presence was sufficiently luminous that the anonymous presence of Christ shone through and touched her—even though neither she nor her analyst were aware of that hidden Presence that was part of their encounter. This is how it is with all encounters. Remember the words of Jesus: When even two or three of you are gathered together, I am in your midst.[4]

🖉 I suggested in this chapter that transformation requires presence and encounter. It seems to me that, as powerful as ideas and words can be, they are ultimately not transformational apart from a relationship, a meeting. I would not be an author if I did not believe that such a meeting can occur through the medium of a book—provided the author brings enough of self to the table that there is genuine presence. What do you think as you reflect on transformational encounters you have had with authors through books or people in the absence of face-to-face meetings?

🖉 Dreams are another category of indirect encounters. Many people speak of dreams as being at the root of awakenings that subsequently flowered into transformation. What does this suggest to you about the potential value of paying attention to dreams?

🖉 Reread my imaginative rendering of the encounter of the two disciples and the risen but unrecognized Christ, or read the account in Luke 24:13–25. Allow your imagination to fill in the missing details. Join with this little group as they walk along. Notice the dusty road and feel the heat of the sun. Be with the two disciples—or perhaps be one of them. Notice your annoyance when the stranger approaches you and seems oblivious to the events you have been discussing, which seem to you to be so momentous. Watch the stranger and notice how easily his identity is missed. Then notice what happens when he breaks the loaf of bread, prays, and passes you a piece of it. Notice what it is like to have your eyes opened. Now that's awakening!

13

REAL PRESENCE, MYSTICAL ENCOUNTERS

I f Christ is somehow anonymously present in all encounters, it seems important to notice the situations in which that presence is more clear and direct. This brings us to the heart of what has usually been described as sacramental or Eucharistic theology and to the factious debate that has resulted in the Christian church being fragmented by the differing answers to the question of what exactly is going on in these encounters. Roman Catholic and Eastern Orthodox Christians speak in terms of the real physical presence of Christ in the Eucharistic elements, while Protestants understand this presence in more spiritual terms, and Anglicans affirm the truth of both understandings.

But perhaps this long-standing debate has missed what I take to be the most important point. Rather than try to explain these mysteries, it seems to me that the crucial thing is to learn how to open ourselves to experiencing them more regularly and deeply. I am content, therefore, to leave the debate over the possible special advantages of the Eucharistic sacrament to theologians. My own interest is how to access real presence through the sacramental possibilities of everyday life.

◊

The truth is that we have brushes with the Divine every day but simply fail to notice the presence of Christ. We feel that if only we had lived in first-century Palestine it would have been so much easier; but most of those who met Jesus failed to recognize Christ. There seems, therefore, to be little reason to think we would have been any different.

Jesus said that he is with us every day, waiting to meet us—present in every hungry person we feed, every thirsty person we give a drink of water. Every day that passes, we meet him, but we fail to recognize him. However, if we are attentive to the movements within our spirit, we will notice stirrings that alert us to that fact that we are in the real presence of Christ. Using the language of the early twentieth-century theologian Rudolf Otto, we might speak of them as responses to *numinous encounters*.

Several things characterize numinous encounters. Usually, they do not feel religious or even spiritual. Because of this, people who are religious, or who are seeking spiritual or religious experience, often do not notice them. If we are attentive, however, we will notice that usually they are accompanied by an affective intensity that we might call a "shudder of the soul." Otto described this as a mixture of two things—what he called *mysterium tremendum* and *mysterium fascinosum*.[1] We are torn between fear and fascination. It's the classic approach / avoidance dilemma. We can't turn our eyes away, yet we can't look directly. So we experience a shudder of the soul.

I believe that these experiences are much more common than we think. Because I have come to realize that they possess unique healing and integrative potential, I have always made attending to them central to my psychotherapy and spiritual accompaniment. I watch for them in dreams and in the experience of those I accompany on an inner journey, particularly in their experience with me when we are together. Let me share one example that arose in the context of psychotherapeutic engagement.

In his early twenties, John was probably the most anxious young person I have ever treated. Nearly crippled with social anxiety, talking to me was extraordinarily difficult for him. But his motivation for assistance in getting past his internal blocks to deep human encounter was so strong that he entered psychotherapy and worked as hard in it as anyone I have ever known.

For the first ten sessions, he never once made eye contact with me. He sat in a far corner of the room with his head down and his eyes covered by long hair that conveniently flopped over his face. He spoke haltingly and with run-on sentences that were filled with qualifications about not being sure if what he was saying was accurate or other similar expressions of his self-doubt.

The eleventh session was quite different. As he entered my office, I saw for the first time something other than anxiety. He seemed caught up in inner torment. Sitting in silence for three or four minutes, he slowly began to sob. Then his sobbing became a howl of anguish. Ten minutes into the session, he had still not said a word to me. Then, as his sobbing began to subside, he wiped his face with his sleeve and looked directly into my eyes and said, "I am afraid that if I tell you what I am experiencing, you will think I am crazy." I told him that I didn't expect that to be the case because in this moment my experience of him was that he was more present and integrated than I had ever previously seen him. I told him that we should set aside attempts to evaluate or even try to understand his experience and that he should simply continue to be present to it—and then, when he was ready, to tell me about it. He said nothing for another minute or two, turning his eyes away from me and returning to an inner focus. Then, looking at me again, he stated, without hesitation or qualification, that he had just touched the pain of the world. Not surprisingly, this was a turning point in his therapy. I never told him that I thought that what happened was a numinous experience. But I did treat it as a sacred encounter. I told him that the meaning of this experience would likely become clearer over time. And it did. Over the next few sessions, he came to realize that the pain of the world was on the edges of his consciousness all the time and that his avoidance of touching it was because he feared being consumed by it. This, he came to realize, was the reason for his anxiety.

Not all numinous encounters are as dramatic as this. Often they are so ordinary and subtle that they are easily overlooked. But as I watch for them, I have come to believe that most people have had at least one such brush with the Wholly Other at some point in their lives.

One of the most consistent features of these brushes with the Divine is that we almost always experience them as something that is totally outside and beyond our selves. This generally has a humbling effect in that it relativizes the ego by confronting us with realities much grander than our small ego-lives. Rather than making us feel larger and grander (an inflated ego), we feel more whole (an integrated ego). This was John's experience. And thankfully for him, paying attention to this encounter opened a door to allow this to be the first stage of a profoundly transformational awakening.

Numinous encounters may be more common than we think, but they do not form a stable part of everyday life. And in them,

Christ's presence in the encounter is still anonymous. However, some encounters with Christ are less anonymous and are, consequently, harder to miss. These would normally be called mystical experiences, and they are not restricted to saints, monks, or spiritual giants. In fact, once again, a life spent in dialogue with people about their inner experience has convinced me that there are many more people who have had mystical experiences than who think of themselves as mystics.

Mystical experiences are, for example, quite common among children who have been abused—regardless of whether or not they have any religious background or experience. Often such children have told me of encounters with angels, Jesus, or God; frequently these encounters happened during the actual abuse. Sometimes I have heard of these experiences decades after the fact and, at that point, also heard reports of how they have helped the person survive. Often it also gave them a deep and persistent inner sense of connection to God, even if God was nowhere on their horizon before the mystical encounters.

I also find that when asked about numinous encounters, many adults without either traumatic history or any significant psychopathology report experiences that are clearly mystical. Generally, they are remembered for the rest of their lives and remain as vivid as if they had just occurred. Often, they have the quality of a vision—that is, something that occurred while they were awake but that had a dreamlike quality to it. Maria described her vision in the following words:

> The vision came to me as I was lying on my bed preparing to go to sleep. My nighttime routine at that point of my life was to lie on top of the covers and think about my day before then getting under the covers, turning out the lights, and falling asleep. Usually, I just let my mind wander over the events of the day. But this night, in the midst of doing so, I suddenly saw myself walking in a wonderful, lush garden. I was startled. I thought I

was dreaming, but then, sitting up and looking around, I realized that I was awake and had not yet fallen asleep.

Somewhat calmed by sitting up and looking around, I once again allowed my eyes to shut. Immediately, I was back in the garden. But now it was different. Rather than looking at the scene, now I was in it. I was experiencing it. I felt a deep sense of peace. I found the garden wonderfully comforting, I could even say enchanting. Suddenly, I noticed a man standing by a bridge over a small stream in front of me. He seemed to be waiting for me, and he was watching me as I walked toward the bridge. He had a gentle welcoming smile on his face that made me wonder if I knew him, or if he knew me. I was very attracted to the warmth of his gaze and wanted to run toward him. But I was also afraid. Something in me held back and made it hard to even look at him. I shifted my eyes away, but each time I glanced back at him, his gaze seemed to have remained on me. Normally, this would bother me, but the warmth of his smile reassured me, and somehow I knew that everything was going to be okay. The closer I came to him, the more I released the anxieties that I seemed to have carried into the garden. The closer I came, the more I forgot myself and felt just caught up in him. Even in the dream, I remember wondering if he was God. I assumed he must be because I can't remember ever before feeling such peace.

That experience happened over ten years ago, but it was as if it was just ten minutes ago. And the sense that everything would be ultimately okay has never left me. That's why I have to believe that it was God. God came to me in that dream and gave me a gift that has never left me.

Dreams and visions share an alteration of normal consciousness, and this is why they are so frequently the context of mystical encounters. We leave no space for such encounters in normal consciousness, so they have to creep into the spaces at the edges of normal consciousness through dreams and visions. Coming to us in those places does not make the experience any less real or valid than if they came to us in normal consciousness. They are encounters, and lurking either in the background or foreground of all encounters is the Christ who makes encounter possible and potentially transformational.

Often, as in the case of Maria's vision, Christ is still disguised. But it's a poor disguise that reveals as much as it hides. However, mystical experiences are not cryptic messages that must be decoded and interpreted. Instead, they should be taken as a whole and listened to through the lens of the impact they have on us. It's the gift that they carry that reveals the identity of the giver—regardless of whether the identity of the giver of the gift is recognized or not.

Another thin place in which we can often encounter the real presence of Christ is through art. In his book *Real Presences*,[2] George Steiner argues that God is a real presence in art that touches us—whether it is a poem, painting, or musical composition, and regardless of whether or not the subject matter is explicitly religious. In other words, he argues that a transcendent reality is the ground of all genuine art, and that reality is the real presence of God. Great art, he argues, is always religious in nature, spiritual in its impulses, transcendent in its meaning, and mysterious in its force.[3]

This is, of course, the same presence that many of us encounter so powerfully in nature. We could use the same words to describe the encounter with the transcendent that is the presence we might experience while walking in the woods, hiking in the mountains, or sitting by a stream—an experience that is spiritual in its impulses, transcendent in its meaning, and mysterious in its force and is, therefore, always ultimately religious in its nature.

All encounters—with other people, with our own depths, or with nature—are mediated by Presence, and that presence is the being of Christ. While this presence is often anonymous, it shouldn't be any surprise that every now and then the cloak of anonymity slips off and we recognize the Christ who stands before us and with us. It is only a small step from this to recognizing this as the same Christ who is within us.

Pausing
—— *to Ponder* ——

Take some time to notice your own encounters with Christ—both anonymous and possibly more direct.

- First, recall any dreams that you may still remember that had a haunting quality to them that simply won't let you forget them. The content may or may not be religious. Just pay attention the encounter. Allow the dream to re-form in your memory and imagination and be present to the Presence that you encountered in the dream.

- Consider whether or not you have had any experiences that I described as numinous encounters, and watch for these in the future. It's amazing how much more frequent they become when you are paying attention!

- Consider whether you have had any explicitly mystical experiences. If you have, honor the experience and the Giver of the experience by reflecting on them once again.

- Notice your experience of the lurking real presence in your encounters with art that speaks to you.

- Finally, reflect on your brushes with the Divine as you experience the natural world in all its fierceness and beauty. This, too, is an encounter with the real presence of God.

14

ENCOUNTERING
DIVINE PRESENCE

Presence is the link between the divine and human realms. Ordinary consciousness distorts the closeness of these two realms and results in our feeling that there is a great chasm between them. But, in truth, the human and divine spheres of life interpenetrate and are inseparable. The sacred and secular are one single fabric of life. The incarnation means that matter really matters. The Eternal Spirit chose to materialize! This is the Christ mystery. God is in the business of connecting matter and spirit. The incarnation makes all the difference in the world!

Presence is, therefore, a doorway through the thin places of life, but all of life is fundamentally thinner than we experience. Again, it's our lack of awareness that is the problem. So often we see only materiality and fail to notice that Spirit interpenetrates it. Presence makes us aware of the thin places in which we walk and live. It is the threshold through which we pass to transform the ordinary into the extraordinary.

Presence always stands in relation to Being itself. This is what makes presence possible and is certainly what makes it transformational. Eckhart Tolle describes this link in the following way:

> Being is the eternal, ever-present One Life beyond the myriad forms of life that are subject to birth and death. However, Being is not only beyond but also deep within every form as its innermost invisible and indestructible essence. This means that it is accessible to you now as your own deepest self, your true nature. But don't seek to grasp it with your mind. Don't try to understand it. You can know it only when the mind is still. When you are present, when your attention is fully and intensely in the Now, Being can be felt, but it can never be understood mentally.[1]

The price of admission to the presence of God is presence to your own self. Or, we could say, the price of admission to the presence of God is simply presence. For in presence, we are in the Sacred Presence, since all presence is simply slipping into the presence of the One who is Presence.

◊

The quest to encounter Divine Presence is central to the Judeo-Christian tradition. Knowing God means knowing God's presence, not merely having beliefs or ideas about God.

In Judaism, the term for God's presence is *Shekhinah*. In Hebrew, this word means "dwelling" or "presence," *Shekhinah* coming to mean the dwelling place of the Divine Presence. Originally, the *Shekhinah* was the temple. Imagine, therefore, how devastating it was for first-century Jews when, in 70 CE, the Romans destroyed the temple. The loss was much more than the loss of a place of worship. It was the loss of the *Shekhinah*—the Divine Presence. The solution to this loss came slowly, but what emerged was an understanding of the Torah being the place of Divine Presence. The holy place of Judaism was no longer a building but a book. *Shekhinah* was to be found in the communal study and discussion of the Torah. This became the central practice of Judaism and the thing that kept Judaism alive after the destruction of the temple.

In the New Testament, Divine Presence is found in the body of Christ—not the physical body of Jesus but the community of those whose lives are centered in Christ. Recall again the words of Jesus—where two or three are gathered in my name, I am in their midst.[2] Although Christians easily slip into associating Divine Presence with churches, we, like Jews, have a theology that states that Presence is most singularly associated with the gathering of the people of the community of faith. As if to underscore the fact that this is now the *Shekhinah*—the place of Divine Presence—the New Testament tells us that this community of faith is the very body of Christ.[3]

This tells us something very important about the communal nature of the spiritual journey. We shouldn't expect to find God and experience God's presence on our own. First and foremost, Divine Presence is to be found in community—in the spaces between and among individuals as they journey together.

Because our very being is an emanation of Divine Being, and because we are made in the image of God, we as individuals also carry Divine Presence within us. Similarly, the world is the body of God and also carries God's presence. Everything that exists is a container for Divine Presence, but the special place where Presence is to be found is in relationships—in the small and large groups of those who journey together and who meet each other in "I-Thou" encounters.

Apart from looking for God in the wrong places and failing to recognize where Divine Presence is most dependably found, another barrier to encountering Presence comes from our faulty expectations. Because our views of God are so anthropomorphic, our expectations are shaped by our experience of encounters with other humans. But God is a spirit, and even though God has come to us in an embodied form, God remains a spirit. God is not simply personal. The Divine Self is transpersonal—not impersonal, but not simply personal. Relationships with God will always be different from relationships with best friends or lovers. People use these metaphors to describe the Divine / human encounter, but, like any metaphor, they obscure as much as they reveal.

Since God is qualitatively different from any other reality in existence, God must be known in a way qualitatively different from our knowing of all other realities. While knowing finite realities involves grasping or comprehending them, God must be known as That Which Lies Beyond All Comprehension. This is what it means to speak of God as Ultimate Mystery, the Wholly Other, or Transcendent.

Yet the mystery that is God is also the core of the mystery of personhood. Consequently, the possibility of human knowing of Ultimate Reality lies in the fact that humans are a reflection of this reality that is remarkably similar to its source. All personal knowing is based in likeness. We can truly know only that which we already resemble in some important way. This possibility lies in the human soul where we retain traces of our origin. The ground of our being is the Ground of Being.

Humans are intimately connected to God because, in some mysterious way, the human soul contains something similar to, possibly even identical with, God. Humans are a unique expression of this reality. The depths of the human soul mirror the depths of Spirit. There is a place in the depths of our souls in which Ultimate Reality alone can dwell and in which we dwell in Ultimate Reality. The nameless depths in us mirror the nameless depth in God. Human mystery is an echo of Ultimate Mystery, but the key to knowing human mystery is knowing the Ultimate Mystery that is God. And the key to knowing the Ultimate Mystery is meeting God in the depths of the human soul.

There is a reason for the similarity in English of the words "mystery" and "mysticism." Encountering Divine Presence will always occur within the veil of mystery. In this place, we see as though through a dark glass. Neither our senses nor reason will ever be able to make sense of what we can encounter. The knowing that results from that encounter is real but is its own form of knowing. Don't expect it to be like sensory or rational knowing. To do so is to confuse matter and spirit. Spirit and matter may interpenetrate, but spirit is never reducible to matter. This is why Scripture tells us that God's ways are not our ways, for God is spirit and we are human.[4]

Mysticism is not primarily about esoteric knowledge or experience. It is all about presence. The primary concern of the mystics has always been knowing the unknowable God. Mystics recognize that the knowing of God that counts is the knowing that comes through encounter in presence. They know that because God is in everything and everything is in God, everything that exists bears traces of Divine Presence. But they realize that the knowing of this Presence is unlike the knowing of anything that we encounter through our senses or rationality.

If, as I have suggested, God is present within each encounter and present to all who are themselves present, God is not as far off or inaccessible as we might fear. Indeed, God is closer to us than we could ever imagine. As Meister Eckhart put it, "God is nearer to me than I am to myself; my existence depends on the nearness and presence of God."[5]

How can we recognize that it is this mysterious God we are encountering if the meeting always happens in twilight? We can do this by noticing several things. The first is that any authentic encounter with God will always be transformational. Jacob emerged from a night of wrestling with God with a limp but also with a new name and a new identity.[6] Saul also needed a new name to reflect his equally new identity after his encounter with God on the Damascus Road.[7] No one escapes from an encounter with Divine Presence unchanged.

Another sign that the encounter is with God is that it always results in a larger, not a smaller, self. Encountering Divine Presence always gives us a vocation. It sends us out into the world with a mission, and the motive behind that mission will always be love. Authentic encounters with God always leave the soul alight, move it to tenderness, and lead to an increase in love.

The mystics add a number of other criteria that attest to the validity of an encounter with God. The most practical of these, I think, is the method of discernment taught by St. Ignatius of Loyola. Ignatius speaks of the importance of attending to the subtle and easily ignored—but crucially important—movements in our spirits that are at the core of spiritual discernment. You may, for example, notice that when your heart is turned to God and you are aware of Divine Love, you are filled with a sense of deep peace and wellbeing or, possibly, a sense of vitality and an impulse to live life more fully and with more passion. "Consolation" is the name Ignatius gave to such feelings that come as gifts of God's gracious presence. It is the way our souls light up when we turn toward God and find ourselves aligned in our depths with God.

However, once you begin to become aware of these feelings that come from having your face turned toward God, you will also notice an entirely opposite set of feelings—*desolation*. These are the feelings that you will notice if you prayerfully attend to what happens in your depths when you turn away from God. You may, for example, notice yourself becoming more self-preoccupied, negative, drained of energy, or irritable. What is happening to you is that your soul is shriveling because what you are experiencing is the early indication that you are on a downward spiral of death. Everyone experiences both consolation and desolation in unique ways, but the presence of these markers can help us know that our faces are either open and toward God or closed and turned away from God.

These markers are also of inestimable value in discerning the true nature of any spiritual encounter. If you encounter God, even though you may limp, there will be a spring in your step because you will sense life flowing through you. You will feel alive and whole, and it is from this new wholeness that your new sense of mission emerges. If, however, you have touched something counterfeit, you will experience the sense of desolation that comes from going against, not with, the stream that is the flow of the Spirit of God—the One who is drawing you and all of creation back to your Source.[8]

If, as I have suggested, there is nothing of more value in life than presence and encounter, the reason this is so is the Presence that is behind all presence and lurking at the edges of all encounters. This is what makes presence and encounter sacraments of everyday life.

For many years, I was an elder in the Presbyterian church. While there are many wonderful parts of that tradition, one thing that always mystified me was why Presbyterians are so afraid of receiving Communion frequently enough that it could become common and ordinary. To keep it special, many Presbyterian churches celebrate communion as infrequently as four times a year. I agree that the sacramental elements of Christian life and faith are special. But my longing to make that specialness a more regular part of my life was one of several reasons that ultimately led me to change brands and become an Anglican. Now I can receive the Eucharist daily if I wish. But far from becoming less special, it is now infinitely more meaningful.

The sacraments are the means of grace that allow us to access Divine Presence. How wonderful that one of these sacraments is so common and ordinary that it is available any time or any day, anywhere. For in every act of presence, the Divine Presence is the background that makes my presence possible. And in every encounter, I can encounter the Christ who is present in the other, in me, and in and among us. This is the mystery and great joy of the sacramental possibility of presence and encounter, and it is a mystery that we can experience in everyday life through presence and encounter!

Thanks be to God!

Pausing
to Ponder

- Consider the closeness or distance between the Divine and human realms in your experience. How thin is the place in which you live your life? What possibilities for closing the gap between the Divine and human realms do you sense in presence and encounter?

- Where do you most directly and powerfully experience Divine Presence?

- Notice any ways that your view of God and the expectations and approach to encountering God may be overly anthropocentric. There is nothing to fear in letting your view of God shift from the personal to the transpersonal. Remember, God is personal but also more than personal. Consider how you can make more space for mystery in your knowing and relating to God.

- Finally, reflect on your encounters with God in the light of the criteria I suggested in this chapter. How might you want to qualify, add to, or change what I suggested?

NOTES

Preface

1. Martin Buber, *I and Thou*, 2nd ed., trans. R. Gregory Smith (Edinburgh: T&T Clark, 1958), 25.

Chapter 1

1. Mark 1:21–28.
2. Ralph Harper, *On Presence* (Philadelphia: Trinity Press International, 1991), 7.
3. Martin Heidegger, *Being and Time* (New York: Harper, 1962).
4. Exodus 3:1–5.
5. John O'Donohue, *Anam Cara* (New York: Harper Perennial, 2004), xvi.

Chapter 2

1. Sigmund Freud, *Three Essays on the Theory of Sexuality* (New York: Basic Books, 1962), 90n1.
2. St. John of the Cross, *Dark Night of the Soul*, http://www.ccel.org/browse /bookInfo?id=john_cross/dark_night
3. Matthew 27:46.
4. Kabir Helminski, ed., *The Rumi Collection: An Anthology of Translations of Mevlana Jalaluddin Rumi* (Boston and London: Shambhala, 2000), 146.
5. John O'Donohue, *To Bless the Space between Us* (New York: Doubleday, 2008), 45.

Chapter 3

1. For years, I have used this exercise to fall asleep at night or to go back to sleep if I experience early awakening. I have also taught this method to many others

who report finding it very valuable as a way of dealing with insomnia. The reason it works is simply that thoughts, which are what keep us awake when we are tired but unable to sleep, cannot coexist with presence.

2. Eckhart Tolle, *The Power of Now* (Novato, CA: New World Library, 1999).

3. John O'Donohue, *Anam Cara: A Book of Celtic Wisdom* (New York: HarperCollins, 1997), 15–16.

4. Simone Weil, *Gravity and Grace*, trans. Emma Craufurd (New York: Routledge & Kegan Paul, 1987), 106.

5. Quoted by William Ralph Inge, *Light, Life, and Love: Selections from the German Mystics of the Middle Ages* (London: Methuen, 1904), Kindle ebook, published by Project Gutenberg, location 600.

Chapter 4

1. Sallie McFague, *The Body of God: An Ecological Theology* (Minneapolis: Fortress Press, 1993).

2. http://www.spiritualpaths.net/mystical-experience-or-unitive-seeing-by -cynthia-bourgeault/.

3. Exodus 33:20. See also John 1:18.

4. William Ralph Inge, *Light, Life and Love: Selections from the German Mystics of the Middle Ages* (London: Methuen, 1904), Kindle ebook, published by Project Gutenberg, location 156–57.

Chapter 5

1. For purposes of this discussion, the terms *meditation* and *contemplation* can be used interchangeably—at least when *meditation* is used to refer to something other than thoughtful pondering. *Contemplation* has been the preferred term in Christian spiritual practice and is the one I will generally use unless I wish to distinguish contemplation from meditation.

2. http://www.ccel.org/ccel/lawrence/practice.

3. Anthony de Mello, *Anthony de Mello: Writings* (Maryknoll, NY: Orbis Books, 1999), 78.

4. Ibid., 88.

5. Ibid., 15.

6. David G. Benner, *Opening to God* (Downers Grove, IL: InterVarsity, 2010).

Chapter 6

1. Slightly complicating this is the fact that some people unconsciously seek out others who allow them to reenact the dynamics of their abuse. Freud called this the repetition compulsion.

2. Sigmund Freud, "Recommendations to Physicians Practicing Psycho-Analysis," in *The Standard Edition of the Complete Psychological Works of Sigmund Freud*, ed. James Strachey, vol. 12 (1911–13) (New York, NY: W. W. Norton & Company, 1976), 110–20.

3. See David G. Benner, *Soulful Spirituality* (Grand Rapids: Brazos, 2011) for more extended discussion of the relationship between body, spirit, and soul.

Chapter 7

1. W. R. Bion, *Attention and Interpretation: A Scientific Approach to Insight in Psycho-Analysis and Groups* (Rome: Armando, 1973).
2. Matthew 15:13–14.
3. 1 Corinthians 13:12.

Chapter 8

1. Acts 17:28.
2. Genesis 2:7.
3. Mark 1:27.
4. Hebrews 12:29.
5. Mark 5:1–9.
6. Martin Buber, *I and Thou*, 2nd ed., trans. R. Gregory Smith (Edinburgh: T&T Clark, 1958).

Chapter 9

1. See, for example, Belle Linda Halpern and Kathy Lubar, *Leadership Presence* (New York: Gotham Books, 2004); Peter Senge, C. Otto Scharmer, Joseph Jaworski, and Betty Sue Flowers, *Presence: Human Purpose and the Field of the Future* (New York: Crown, 2008).
2. See David G. Benner, *Spirituality and the Awakening Self* (Grand Rapids: Brazos, 2012) for more on levels of consciousness and their relationship to awakening and transformation.
3. Eckhart Tolle, *A New Earth: Awakening to Your Life's Purpose* (New York: Dutton, 2005), 6.
4. John O'Donohue, *Eternal Echoes: Celtic Reflections on Our Yearning to Belong* (New York: Harper Perennial, 2000), 68.
5. Matthew 4:18–22.
6. Matthew 7:15.

Chapter 10

1. Exodus 3.
2. Matthew 25:40–45; Luke 6:17–49.

Chapter 11

1. For more of the story of my friend Dr. Donald Woodside, see http://www.drdavidgbenner.ca/meditation-and-contemplative-prayer-an-interview/.
2. Thich Nhat Hanh, *Buddha and Christ* (New York: Riverhead Trade, 2007), 9.

Chapter 12

1. An imaginative engagement with the story presented in Luke 24:13–25.
2. Matthew 18:20.

3. I have also shared something of this woman's story in chapter 3 of *The Gift of Being Yourself* (Downers Grove, IL: InterVarsity, 2004).

4. Matthew 18:20.

Chapter 13

1. Rudolf Otto, *The Idea of the Holy* (London: Oxford University Press, 1923).

2. George Steiner, *Real Presences* (Chicago: University of Chicago Press, 1991).

3. This is an adaptation of the conclusion of Eva Hoffman in her *New York Times* review of the first edition of George Steiner's book, *Real Presences*. Her book review can be found at http://www.nytimes.com/1989/08/09/books/books-of-the-times-an-engaged-humanist-pleads-art-s-cause.html.

Chapter 14

1. Eckhart Tolle, *The Power of Now* (Novato, CA: New World Library, 1999), 10.

2. Matthew 18:20.

3. 1 Corinthians 12:27.

4. Isaiah 55:8.

5. Meister Eckhart, *Christian Ethereal Classics*, "Meister Eckhart's Sermons, 'The Nearness of the Kingdom,'" location 20/21, http://www.ccel.org/ccel/eckhart/sermons.v.html.

6. Genesis 32:21–34.

7. Acts 9.

8. For a fuller discussion of the psychology, theology, and spirituality of these rules of discernment, see chapter 7, "Developing a Discerning Heart," of my *Desiring God's Will: Aligning Our Heart with the Heart of God* (Downers Grove, IL: InterVarsity, 2005).